Praise for

I've long been a fan of Walter Bargen's poetry, but in these short prose pieces he surpasses himself. They're lovely and subtle, brilliant and strange. He has a keen sense for the surreal and the absurd but, unlike lesser writers, he never retreats into *mere* surrealism or absurdity. . . . In *The Feast*, Bargen recreates characters in delightful, startlingly modern ways. He is one of the Midwest's most brilliant—and underappreciated—writers at work today.

—Kevin Prufer

In *The Feast*, Walter Bargen has generated a cosmology that ricochets between eschatology and creation, and he's fostered a world that simultaneously dies and is reborn out of the chaos of consciousness. . . . History is not a nightmare from which Bargen is trying to awake; it is a sea of contingency, congruence and limitless possibility into which Bargen dives headlong.

—Gary Young

...This book is hugely ambitious, original, affecting, and at many points, extraordinarily powerful.

—*St. Louis Post-Dispatch*

I have trouble deciding which myth Bargen has more fun with: the mythical heroes or the myth of poetry and where the line is drawn between them. The longer he dances on that line, the more the reader benefits.

—*Sentence*

When language is true as it is in these poems, we are redeemed.

—*Redactions*

Also by Walter Bargen

Fields of Thenar
Mysteries in the Public Domain
Yet Other Waters
Rising Waters
The Vertical River
At the Dead Center of Day
Water Breathing Air
Harmonic Balance
The Body of Water
Remedies for Vertigo
West of West

the FEAST

prose poem sequences

Walter Bargen

Art by Mike Sleadd

BkMk Press
University of Missouri-Kansas City

BkMk Press
University of Missouri-Kansas City
5101 Rockhill Road
Kansas City, Missouri 64110
(816) 235-2558 (voice)/(816) 235-2611 (fax)
bkmk@umkc.edu, www.umkc.edu/bkmk

Financial assistance for this project has been provided by the Missouri Arts Council, a state agency.

Cover design, author photo by Mike Sleadd (www.inkguy.com)

Production staff: Ben Furnish (managing editor), Susan L. Schurman (assistant managing editor), Ryan Cunningham, Matt Ehrhorn, Lisieux Huelman, Jessica Hylan, Emily Iorg, Karen I. Johnson, Elizabeth Gromling

Library of Congress Cataloguing-in-Publication Data

Bargen, Walter.
      The feast: prose poem sequences/Walter Bargen ; art by Mike Sleadd
      p. cm.
ISBN 1-886157-39-1
      I. Prose poems, American.
PS3552.A6162 F43 2003
811/.54 21

                              2003012178

This book is set in Palatino type.
Second printing, 2008

for m. b. r.

❧Acknowledgments❧

Parts of this manuscript have appeared in the following magazines:

Barnabe Mountain Review	Garden of Delights
Delmar Magazine	Night Elegies
Georgia Review	Being Its Time
	The Black and Blue Book
	Either/And
Furious Fictions	Shaking Yggdrasil
International Quarterly	The Sickness of Buildings
	Giant Dirty Trick
	Nine Lives on the
	Western Front
New Novel Review	Born Under Glass
	Odysseus in Springfield
Quarter After Eight	The Unnatural Daughter
	Macchiato
	The Unseasonal Town
	Belly of the Beast
	Avian Cusine
	Lost Crew
	Odyesseus Skips the
	Revolution
	Sea of Us
	Sea of Love
River City	Keelhauled
Spoon River Quarterly	Rain of Shoes

"Nine Lives On The Western Front" was a finalist in the International Quarterly Crossing Boundaries Awards, 1995.

"In the Belly of the Beast" was winner of the *Quarter After Eight* New Prose Award, 1996.

"Delphic Chicken" and "Occupations" appear in the anthology *Third Stream: Writing Boundaries* from Lonesome Traveler Press.

"The Rising Flocks" appeared in the 1998 Icarus Foundation winner's anthology.

❧Contents❧

Some Doubts

1

. . . between two worlds, one dead,

The other powerless to be born.

Matthew Arnold

2

. . . the hero lives on; even his downfall was

merely a pretext for achieving his final birth.

R. M. Rilke

3

and I put it to my lips

and kept it there a long while–

the blood of love against my lips.

C. P. Cavafy

4

I know how to be abased . . . . Everywhere and in all things I have learned

both to be full and to be hungry, both to abound and to suffer need.

Philippians 4:12

5

What's never known is safest. . .

Dylan Thomas

Belly of the Beast

*To be properly expressed a thing must proceed from
within, moved by its form.*
    –Meister Eckhart

*Every man takes the limits of his field of vision for
the limits of the world.*
    –Arthur Schopenhauer

Before the Beginning

This is what happens when he stands face to face with no, and no the true genius of the world. No, he won't sit on the potty, and so he sits wrapped in his mess for the rest of the day. No, he won't struggle with putting on his galoshes on a rainy morning, and so he walks to school barefoot, all the other kids laughing. No, he won't stand on the chair, lean among the flowers to kiss the face of someone who once loved to playfully cheat him at cards and torment him in other small delicious ways, then his frightened face is shoved up against death. No, he won't give the older boys his jacket, and after school is chased all the way home, barely staying ahead of the heavy swinging belt buckles. No, he won't eat his broccoli or spinach, or anything green that looks like the squashed insides of a caterpillar, and he falls asleep at the table, then falls out of the chair. No, he cannot say no, but he does. No, he won't go to the barbarous city of Nineveh, but instead heads for Tarsh-ish, across a storm-riddled sea where he draws the short straw and is thrown overboard for God-only-knows-what-reason, and ends up living inside a great fish. Yes, no is the genius of the world.

No-Jon-Ah

No one notices even on days when he stands in the cashier's line at Wal-Mart, holding a water-filled plastic bag with bright swimming things that he is a man who lives inside a fish. Actually, he lives in a house he carved out of the inside of a living fish. He can't remember how long he has sat at the one table built from a giant fish scale. He rarely opens his eyes anymore, not because there isn't any light, a fish oil lamp flickers in the middle of the horny-scaled table, but because he feels better not watching what passes below the invisible floor of his rib-roofed house. His eyelids slammed shut when he thought he heard cries for help pass below him. The guttering flame from his burning blubber, scraped from the walls of his fishy house and poured into the seashell lamp, only cast gurgling shadows. He can see nothing but the viscous percolation, the amorphous dissolving of sea into fish.

He is left with only the faint echo of something, the insidious scratching and scrapping of hermit crabs making homes inside his ears. He can't say if what he thinks he heard was yesterday, last week, or years ago. But if it was yesterday, the pain is still sharp enough for him to long for a dust-choked earth. If it was last week, the grief is already being carried away in a stream of memories. If it was years ago, then the tide has continued to rise and he's now awash in a cataclysmic flood, on his last gasp, treading water. He's planning to build a submarine to save all the creatures floundering at this depth. He knows that it is only those of us who can't swim who will save ourselves.

Jonahic Dislocations

When the great fish finally slurped up every corner of the
ocean down to the last drops hidden in the crevices of the
Great Barrier Reef, down to the pools bottomed in the Java
Trench, draining the vast abyssal hills, turning the Yangtze
and Yukon alluvial fans into cracked mudflats, baring the
submerged roots of the Lesser Antilles to the Bahamas and
forming a range of mountains with tropical summits, when at
last the fish sprawled at the mouth of the Amazon as the last
whisper of the longest current slipped between its lips, it lay
sprawled, bug-eyed, gasping, its body bloated and misshapen
by the world's oceans and seas; and Jonah in his fishhouse was
exhausted from frantically plugging the leaks, mopping his
invisible floor, a one-man bucket brigade, as the Atlantic and
Pacific rushed past, the Black Sea and the Baltic, the Mediter-
ranean and Lake Superior.   He was pruned, his skin shriv-
eled, fold after translucent fold submerging into itself. He felt
salted and pickled. The great fish lay unmoving except for
its archaic gills slowly fanning up a dust storm that engulfed
Brazil. It looked as if it swam to the end of the earth.

     Jonah wading waist deep through his rib-roofed
house, trying to keep his table and lamp from floating into a
sopping oblivion, was ready to throw in the towel, when the
fish arched its continent-long back, slapped down its tectonic
plate of a tail and lunged forward, coughing up all that it had
swallowed, making rivers run backward, popping the po-
lar ice caps like just-opened soda bottles, setting the Titanic
down on Broadway in New York City, leaving Jonah beached
on the boardwalk in Bombay. Jonah turned to face the gap-
ing mouth of the great fish. It slithered backward into the sea
and belched. From its fishy breath he heard the rasping of the
thousand-thousand holy names and he dived back into the
dark maw.

fish@net.com

There must have been a great battle, or else his great fish was on fire. Perhaps it had been torpedoed and was soon to sink. Smoke billowed from the maw of its throat. His ribbed cavern blackened. He thought he could hear the blare of trumpets, the irregular thunder of explosions, the gnash and scrape of immense machines grinding together. His rib-roofed house began to choke from acrid odors of burning diesel and flesh. He lay down on his invisible floor, hoping not to die in spasms of coughing. He saw sparks sputter, fly through the air, the silhouettes of men running at each other across a stark, cratered landscape, hysterical men shouting and waving bayonets, then falling into each other's arms and then to their knees, then falling even lower, row after row crushed into the raw, mothering dirt. He shook in amazement, quaked in fear, clung to the sides of his beloved fish, but he couldn't take his eyes off the erupting streaks of light tracing the twisting miles of barbed wire like the nerves of a monstrous dying animal—the mother of all battles. Then the room filled with static. The invisible floor darkened. The battery that he'd salvaged from a crate of floating debris died. The laptop screen glowed a solid gray then blackened. He flipped the switch, the mouse with its wire tail sinking into the sea—the interface finished. He knew for certain, no news is good news. The great fish's stomach rumbled on, devouring history, headed for Omaha Beach and Agincourt.

Whalular *Throbosis*

He lit his shell lamp and held it outside the window. What
was the slow dull throb that at first he attributed to the onset
of a migraine caused by sitting too long in the blubbery dark?
Here in a tower of spiraling narwhal tusks, he could discover,
delineate, pontificate on the ichthyosaural prime mover. He
could contemplate the first-cause and the final-cause throb, the
epistemological throb and the ontological throb, the pain-in-
the-ass throb and the crotch throb, and still not move an inch.

Standing at the window, he saw the inside of his great
fish filling with the heart of a city in need of angioplasty: all
its arteries clotted with traffic, its gleaming headlighted blood
at a near standstill, its lungs black and exhausted, rivers dis-
colored and syrupy, the park trees leafless. He swore not to
chug another bottle of his home-brewed fermenting fish.

But it was no delirium tremor. From this height, high
in the belly, where the ribs curve up into studded-stars, spar-
kling with the remnants of the last backwash of cosmic debris,
up the many rickety rungs of ladders, frayed ropes and tow-
rope-thick varicose veins, along greasy precipitous ledges, that
all led to his bone-roofed hermitage, he could see the present
claiming a broken-down past, struggling toward a whimsical,
consummate future, and then the lights began to fade in one
section after another of the city, a massive power blackout,
a heart attack, the light clotted, and then he realized he was
staring down at the last gulp of phosphorescent red tide and a
night of throbbing indigestion.

Keeping Whale Hours

It really could be. Yes, it really could, and that's what he keeps repeating to himself in admiration of the grand conception. It's the first time in days he has stepped out of his house balanced on its blubbery edge. He descends the kelp and bone ladders. He is whistling the latest pop ditty, heard on the radio before the batteries weakened and the acid bubbled forth, corroding the transistors. Yes, he is on his way, carrying a sheaf of shark fins under his left arm, gripping an air-bladder briefcase, swinging his shell lamp. His shadow leaps forward and back, as if he is in a hurry, bounces up and down, as he swells in importance with each step. He stops in front of each rib and knocks, more than half-expecting it to swing open, his pale knuckles hanging in midair in a gesture of authority. When no one answers, he posts the fin on the calcium-white door and moves on. In fact, for full effect he hangs from each bony arc a deep-sea fish, the one that lights its own way with exaggerated glowing needle-thin teeth and carries its own flesh-waggling neon lure attached to its head. Finished, he sees banks of fin-slapping fluorescent lights stretching down a whale of a hallway. When he reaches the last door that won't ever open and posts the cartilage that will never be read, he realizes that for a moment it was something to do. He turns around and forces himself slowly back up the tiers of swinging ladders and sits down in his rib-roofed house, headquarters for cetacean world tours.

Orpheus Fishlove

For hours he could hear someone wandering far below, kicking at the debris of civilizations: elegant, cracked clay urns, twisted steamship paddle wheels, eye-white bleach bottles, clouded miles of tangled fish nets, tumbled Ionic columns, heavy stone calendars stained with sacrifices, arm- and legless marble statues, chariots, tireless Edsels, windowless Studebakers—the overwrought fever of centuries and the overwrought digestion of a fish's galactic hunger.

It was a man, he was certain of that, the heavy clank and clang, the scrape and rasp, moving immovable objects, searching for something, shoving aside granite griffins and defaced sphinxes, the entire edifice of religions and astrological projections, Hammurabi's Code and the Magna Carta. But it was the words, the first he had heard in years, maybe minutes, he didn't know, time lost and forgotten in this cavernous gut, and the phrases so ethereal, he began to swoon. He cowered below his windowsill, shaking his head in disbelief, now that the hallways of his ears were suddenly drained, soaked corridors dry, his head emptying to a paramecium, then threatening to explode with the melodies that entered and would not leave. The stranger never stopped singing of what he'd lost, the endless search, the repeated failure. Every inch of his pale, flaccid skin ached to be wrapped in the thigh's curve, the arm's heated embrace, the hand's delicate probing and firm stroke.

Listening from his high-house perch, he heard songs blending the murmur of the sea and the murmur of the dead, and he grew afraid. He could see the flicker of the torch that the man held high and the lyre he carried in his other hand. His back was turned as he walked farther away, past pyramids and earthen mounds. The stranger was searching for something else, for an uncivilized love, one with the power to tame three-headed dogs, boil away rivers of forgetfulness, stand an army of spirits at attention against the will of wind. He wanted to tell the stranger he hadn't gone far enough; he needed to go deeper than this junkyard, beyond where even great fish swim, but his voice had drifted off in a corked bottle. When the torch flicked its last spark and the man was out of sight, continuing his journey toward an immense, if not infinite loss, he sat safely behind his dripping blubber walls and again swore devotion to his mute fish, and wept.

Sun Screen

He desperately shields his eyes from the sun. The shade of four fingers isn't enough. Too new out of the flickering dark, he can't see a thing. Placing his palms over his eyes, he stares at X-rays, the surf-jumbled bones of his hands clearly visible to him, delicate as the wings of flying fish, but hardly looking strong enough to hold up the net of his sagging skin. Not to be dragged back by the undertow, he claws at the waves. The gentle rocking of each swell threatens to topple him, as he half-walks, half-scuttles toward the shore.

The light splintering on the green surface spears every exposed inch of his skin. He's an exotic specimen waiting to be collected. He staggers under the glaring blue magnitudes of sky. He passed through hours of the sea's churning labor, the great fish's slow dilation, and the final moment when its throat clamped down and then spewed him forth—his ladders and house finally reaching beyond mere irritant.

His translucent soles shoot the searing heat of the sand up into his knees. He's dazzled by the bright shards of col-ored towels spread over the beach. He quickly stumbles into the shade of an umbrella, where a woman lies, every inch of her exposed, every inch tan. He sits down confused, ready to speak the prophecy of her doom, asking if this is Nineveh, but feeling the primal throb.

Speechless, she stares at this thing that's come from the sea and belongs back under the waves. He's a talking page ripped from an anatomy book: blue veins pulsing under his skin, the shadows of bones rising from the fleshy depths of arms and legs, lips unable to hide the bald grin of teeth. Startled, she answers no, this is North Miami Beach. She introduces herself, Jessabelle, says she sells Mary Kay Cosmet-ics, and knows just the product for his condition. If he agrees to let her use before-and-after photographs for a sales promo-tion, it would be a no-charge consultation. The sea casting up its pastels, the scattered clouds powder puffs, a blush of sky marking the sun, they leave the beach in her pink Cadillac.

Psalm 66

He didn't have to swim a thousand miles—he drove, and now he simply pushes open the building's double doors, steps out onto the cinder-ridden sidewalk, and inhales the decomposing odors of flotsam and jetsam. At this rise in elevation, lined with century oaks, punctuated with an intersection where cars feign stops before speeding on, all the sea would run downhill, unless the hill itself is a slow welling up of sea.

      Before crossing the street, he searches for the flash of scales, a fin flip, the turbulence of a school of tuna roiling the sunstruck surface. The morning-wet whale-back asphalt glistens. Standing on the curb he has nothing to say. He has listened to the doomsayers and the prodigal sons, the assessors and the hedonists, the elected and the lost, and he casts his lot into the depths, crosses through a storm of traffic, and is coughed up into another day of work, a fishy odor lingering on his clothes. A small driftwood picture frame, sitting near a corner of his desk, floats these watery words:

> From the ends of the oceans will I
> cry unto thee,
> when my heart is overwhelmed:
> lead me to the fish that is higher
> than I.

Nine Lives on the Western Front

Paleolithic Conversation

For the first time in over a week, Jonah wakes without pain. His arm moves up to grab the headboard. He lifts himself slowly, expecting the twisting and firing of nerves, thin piercing streams that rap the right side of his head, but this morning it's gone. Relief eases itself into consciousness and begins to break down his defenses. He feels that he has slept more soundly than he can remember, perhaps dreamless because at this moment he can recall nothing. A small elation hovers in front of him. From the edge of the bed, he can see out the window into an immense gray sky and through the trees that have dropped most of their leaves, keeping only a blush of color hanging along scattered branches.

None of this makes sense. He resists such simplicity. Why should he deserve this? He begins to long for the pain that ropes his right shoulder, cinches him tight, jerks him in any direction it wants. How can he accept that he can turn to the right or left, free of the shimmering gown of pain that he wears for almost every occasion? Is that why with his first step—the lifting of his leg, the bending of the knee, the arch rising, the toes preparing to set down—that he finds himself expecting to miss the floor, as if it weren't wide enough or he might not ever reach it. A painless step lasts forever, he thinks, or is he just confused by the intricate shadows cast by the kitchen and bedroom lights? But he should be used to this trellis of dark angles.

By the time he pulls the chair away from the kitchen table it should be late afternoon, but his watch has measured minutes. Between each bite of toast are hours in which he drifts, the light a yellow haze that grows thicker until he is passing through an endless wall, as if he had not bothered to excavate the ancient city he's entering. Finished, he sets the white plate in the sink with its burnt crumbs scraped from one edge of the bread, the hungered punctuation from a Paleolithic conversation. Yet only five minutes have passed.

In the shower, water falls so slowly it evaporates before it touches the tiles. He looks for a place, a stratum of air behind the plastic curtains that remains dry. It's the only explanation for his wrinkled skin and the sand that collects by the drain where it trickles into the dark side of the hourglass. Steaming sand pours down the back of his neck, collects in the small of his spine before it drifts around his feet. He is dry before he is wet. With the towel he wipes away sweat. Dressed, he slips his feet into the wrong shoes. He ties knots that have no hope of holding. He thinks, "I've traded the pains in my shoulder for the pains of living."

Exorcism of the First Spoon

In the pure white light of the kitchen, the dust motes tumble slowly, catching the weak currents of air that rise and fall over the spotless tile counters. The specks cling, like the emperor's new clothes, to young Jonah who has entered looking for something to complete the fort he is building on the floor under the table in the dining room. He chooses a couple of forks, and sticking their tines together, they project like a mouth of sharpened teeth, reminding him of concrete barriers crowded into mountain passes to stop advancing armies. He chooses tall glasses set upside down on their lips to make watchtowers and prisons for whoever dares attack and risk capture. Amid the forest of chairs and behind thick, scarred wooden table legs the enemy waits. He finds an empty cereal box. With scissors he cuts holes in the sides for his defenders, raises it as a wall, and easily tears it up in the explosions he shapes between his hands.

The light entering through the window above the sink inflates the room. The floor rises to meet the ceiling. He finds himself standing on the counter looking down at the immaculate porcelain, how it cradles the blue sponge and gives rise to the monument of chrome faucets. He sees the open drawer. Did he open it and step on the folded towels or did he fly? Either way the cabinets are before him. The possibilities for his fort are multiplied far beyond what he knows.

Up here the air is rarefied. Behind the first door are crystal vases and bowls—this must be where the evil ice king lives. He steals the king's wand to use it to protect his fort. The ice gods will avenge quickly, but he will overpower them with their own magic. The second door is home to the wicked Chinese emperor. He swings it open quickly, grabs what he can, and slams it shut. He's not turned into a spider, though he's not sure what it is he holds, but he'll use it to defend against the wrath of the yellow hordes. The third belongs to the demonic magician. If he is to succeed, he must wait and slip between the floating dust, not touching a single particle in this network of microscopic spies. He takes a deep breath, holds it, turns sideways, and sees the red-faced queen standing in the doorway. He gets down quickly. The war is lost.

The ice king, the Chinese emperor, the magician are in pursuit, but they must wait their turn. He forgot the simplest instrument resting in the utility drawer beside the silverware. He could have used it for a catapult, but now he must place his open hand down on the clean white counter. The immensely cool white counter. His palm feels the smooth grout between the tiles. Love must be a spoon. Love must be a wooden spoon. Love must be a broken wooden spoon. Broken across his knuckles. Surely, love is a river of broken spoons flowing through every room, out the front door, and down every street.

Exhausted Spectrum

They pillage past Jonah's window. He dreams both victor and vanquished, but the final terms for either confuse him. Each morning he wakes to a new wound buried under his sea-glass skin. He's his own museum. Lately his wrists have become crowded, veins snarled and dead end at his heart. His chest, pounded into bruises, can't metamorphose into a deeper purple, or move into a violet beyond sight—his spectrum is exhausted. The endless list of wounds that are failing him: toenails rusted with blood, forearms lacerated like a cat's scratching post, sleep stricken daily from his eyes, yet he returns to see the exploded sheets and the mattress's dull crater.

This morning Jonah works to sit upright. Splinters of sleep pierce his legs, stiffen his fingers. The memories of pain are there and not there. The appendix scar rides above the saddle of his hip, that delicate declivity where a warm breath or touch of lips coils his body back into a feral past. It was twenty-five years before he could bring himself to finger the braided, numb-white skin. This morning with intricate petals of frost spreading over the window, as if a whole army had breathed on the glass, room light muted, there buried in his arm is the ache of knitted calcium, the broken doors of bones knocking, will he never forget the leap from the tree or the bicycle wheel caught in the drainage grate?

Down the street there are friends missing. Years ago they moved to drown themselves in a sea, or fall off a mountain, and they never wrote, breaking the promise they never made. He knows one man melted into his bottle and another tried to save them all and wandered the streets banging into ceilings of people.

The wounds shimmer, the preened feathers of plucked angels. They flutter over the bed waiting for the right moment to land as he lies deep in the wounds of others. He enters the wound of the woman who lies next to him and Jessie moans for another minute of mercy. There are cat fights and scared dogs barking before they finish. There are massacres in fields he tries never to know, bomb blasts in subways that disrupt schedules he's never kept, prison camps without food where he hasn't eaten, methods of torture that scar only the backs of the eye, and tortures that erupt on the inside of his thighs.

On the phone one night, naked, the heat of summer swelling his pores, Jonah talks to a woman whose name he can't remember, although she once opened completely to him. She says things he dare not understand, not because of the other woman she can't see, who now stands naked next to him at that distant moment of conversation, but because he watches Jessie's hand trace the hourglass of her waist down over her hip and reaching deep between legs, parting her own engorged lips, she raises a blood-drenched hand and begins to smear clawed streaks down his chest. Jessie burns spread-fingered prints far back in the caves of his skin. He can hear the crimson fur howl, his skin a dark inside lit by the clotting fury of another life. Under the ceiling light in the middle of the room, his body immersed in wet flames, he holds the receiver up to tongue the conflagration of all their wounds.

A Citrus of Difference

It's the way Jessie serves Jonah orange juice, or that she pours
a glass and serves it to him at all, as he sits at the kitchen table
on a Saturday morning, staring at a plate of muffin crumbs,
the background radio news accounting for last night's disasters.
He knows that his wife is having an affair. He doesn't say
anything to her about what he now knows, and thanks her
for the orange juice. He drinks as if nothing were out of the
ordinary.

Actually, it is later after he has dressed in jeans and
blue work shirt, standing on the porch with a cup of coffee,
staring up into the flickering quilt of fall foliage, that he begins
to doubt his own life, and the possibilities.

Long before the mortgage is up, knots have loosened
and fallen out, and cracks have widened beyond safety on the
porch where he works the afternoon replacing boards. He
hammers the cat's-paw under the rusting nailheads and pulls,
the metal wedded to wood screeches as the shanks are bent
and pried out; they seem to know only the pain of release, so
he stops. The porch is left a maze of long rectangular holes
like the scrolled tunes of an ancient player piano. Each time he
glances over his sweaty shoulder, he sees the tune and hears
the lament. When Jehovah's Witnesses come to preach their
world to him, before they reach the doorbell, one slips and
falls through, twisting an ankle. Now he faces a lawsuit from
God. His wife hires a local handy man to replace the missing
boards.

The next weekend he notices the top blocks of the
chimney are deeply stained. Leaning a ladder against the gut-
ter, he climbs onto the roof, walks a shingled valley cluttered
with twigs, sprouting acorns, rotting leaves, and along a ridge
splotched with lime lichen and moss. He discovers that the
concrete is severely eroded, cracked, crumbling. He returns
from the hardware store with mortar and starts the repairs.
On the roof of a two-story house, he is at treetop and finds
himself thrust into a unrelenting blue sky. He's stuccoed two
sides of the chimney when he sits down on the ridgecap, a leg
on either side, as if a horse has slipped under the house, and

now he is in the saddle. He raises one hand into the sky as if the house were bucking. There is simply too much blue for him to ride into to bother with further repairs. After hours of the TV unattended, his wife comes out and suggests he come down. Jessie calls the local handyman who arrives days later to finish the half-hour job, but charges half-a-day's labor for driving to their house.

The neighbors have noticed the porch, the chimney, and mention these events to his wife, as if both concerned and threatened. Since they never talk directly to each other, or of anything significant, his wife begins to ask small, odd questions that have never needed answering before, such as, why did he part his hair on one side of his head one day, and then on the other the next? He doesn't have an answer that he thinks she will understand. When he stares into the mirror for minutes at a time, staring into his own pupils, staring to see into the well of those tarry pits, Jonah's looking for where it all comes from. He notices that his face shifts like earth during a quake, tilts like a slot machine pushed to win and the lights flashing tilted, so he parts his hair on one side then the other, to keep the blue tectonic plates that radiate from his head balanced.

In the kitchen his wife opens the refrigerator and pulls out the orange-juice pitcher. She mixed the frozen pulp and water six days ago. She pours him another glass. The vitamin C long gone, she wants to get rid of it. For a second time in a month, in their twenty-five years of marriage, Jessie serves him at breakfast. Jonah never asks. She never knows.

The Procession of Pears

Jonah goes back to the foyer among the coats hanging in the wrinkles and dust of their abandonment, and wonders how will they ever again shake loose of their hooks and raise their exalted arms. Back to where the hats find no circumference of thought to settle on, and float, felt and wool unraveled by the moth of emptiness. Back to where the gloves lose their grip and begin to shake, having held up more than is possible, and scarves flutter so slowly no one notices their enfolding grief. Back to where they grow in anonymous piles on the overhead shelf. Back to where the inexplicable display of decaying boxes of boots and shoes, having lost their leather-cracked mates, sit. Where the floor buries itself under the walls that are desperate to forget a thousand thousand leavings, even as the walls sink into the floor relieved to collapse, leaving the foyer to the discarded convulsions of a small family.

Amid the debris of living, Jonah gladly bows down on his knees and empties the box of pears that he harvested. He picked them out of the grass, careful not to be stung by wobbling bees drunk on the decay fallen from bent branches. Near the trees, the evening light turned the fenceposts across the field into candles and the barbed wire into a taut smoke. Led by the dwindling procession of weathered wooden penitents, the pears scattered in the grass are a trail of glowing drops of yellow wax.

Yes, he gladly spreads the pears over the cold foyer floor and examines the skin of each one closely, rolling the sensuous globes in his palm as if ripe evenings were loosening around their worlds, feeling their flesh for firmness, diagnosing blemishes, probing bruises, finally judging the rotten when his fingers penetrate and the brown pulp oozes between them with a soft sweetness. He gladly stays on his knees to save what's left from decay, and once he's done, spreads them out again, because there is no stopping their descent. He carries the crushed, the moldy, the skinless, the weeping, out to the garden where they continue their generous decline. He returns to the foyer—it's the only thing left for him to do.

Nine Lives on the Western Front

At the table in a voice that no longer belongs to her but to this century: echoing down twenty-feet-high sound barriers along the shoulders of freeways; from person to person in unemployment lines, who expect nothing more than the line to be there tomorrow; on street corners where rumors flex their muscles at passing girls and they still fall for it; and in this kitchen steeped with yellow light, Jessie announces the unequivocal success of their failures.

Too quickly, their lives are beyond them and not theirs, herded across borders, walked out into the middle of fields and left there, shoved through doors into unspeakable rooms. Now across from her sits a man, a mere vehicle, her husband, Jonah, whose mother half a century ago became pregnant and married the conquering army of a war-ravaged continent. According to Jessie, he was simply a means to an end, and now she's left with this broken tool to wrench the world back into place. She lifts Jonah's hands, curls his fingers around two empty beer bottles, and points outside. Jessie points to herself; long before amniocentesis, there was the avalanche of her parents' disappointment, wanting a boy, only a boy, then having to face decades of her. The avalanche sweeps across the table to their son sitting between them. He continues to eat, face down to his plate, as if nothing is being said. She demands to know what he thinks he's doing—trying to be like his parents?

Jonah, speechless, recalls a childhood game called hot potato. He sat in a sandbox with friends, one in each corner, throwing something back and forth, a plastic bucket or ball, but instead of a scalding potato, they imagined a hand grenade. He can't remember how they decided that it exploded and which one of them would leap backwards out of the sandbox, arms and legs thrown outward, a human asterisk, or if the shrapnel-shredded flesh was ever more real than a scraped elbow or knee, and exactly how many times they could die before dinner.

Sleep of Angels

Jonah gives the bed wings and arranges them like the blades of a helicopter. Many smaller beds fly through the room. They are plentiful as whining mosquitoes, their wings creating a celestial annoyance. Whoever enters the room is driven mad by visions of perfection, and in order to survive, invents lesser beds, ones with only two wings. These beds take off and land like bombers returning from missions during World War II—Berlin and Dresden. Whole squadrons, trailing sheets of smoke, approach the room's running lights. They crash-land into the nightstand, knocking off the clock and the flight crew's portrait that is always missing one person. They slam into walls already discolored from the leaking engines of an ancient sleep. Some land with only one wheel strut down and spin off the edge of the bed. Some skid on their bellies the length of the mattress before bursting into flames. Another is landed by the tailgunner, the rest of the crew wounded and dying. One bomber lands with no crew at all. This last plane shows no sign of damage, not a single bullet hole. No blood smeared across the control panels or splattered on the windshield. The crew has vanished. This plane sits at the base of the headboard for weeks, everyone afraid to touch it. Finally, it's swept under the bed and never spoken of again.

The dead are so much easier to care for, lined up and counted, smiling under their sheets, still wearing their leather jackets and helmets, recalling how peaceful it was in their oxygen masks, flying above the ceiling and staring down at the rolling clouds. For those crews that must ditch in the sea, the pillowcases open into parachutes, dumping all the tousled heads hidden in their linens. As for the rest that exploded with their targets—factories filled with mothers and fathers— they have already begun free falling, and because guards become prisoners, and prisoners turn into guards, no prisoners are taken. Back in bed, another mission completed, the debriefing over, the damage assessed, the pilots lie back and sleep the sleep of angels.

Armies of Love

He could not help but fall in love though he was not ready for the surrender. Jonah was a soldier and had taken the soldier's oath, so he looked for a way out: a tunnel under the wire, an accent that was not his, his face before he was born. Actually, he didn't need to plan an escape, he was still wandering the desert when he realized this, his uniform stained with grease, blood, and explosions. He was beyond recognition, and with no frontline to defend, no flag to wave, he's left only with a rearguard defense no matter which way he turns.

Even if he'd never been in the desert, his eyes would still sting with sand and flare with irritation, the way tracer bullets are simply trying to locate their death. This is love after all—running into the arms of an explosion, wanting to be shredded by shrapnel, dismembered by mines, to paint the air with Valentines of blood, until there is nothing left of who he is. Still a piece of him walks away. A hero to us all, to be torn apart by our adoration.

He is a soldier of patience. He polishes his rifle for hours—stares down the barrel, aligns the sights, rubs oil onto every part, feels its full weight in his hands, cradles it in his arms, opens the chamber and slides in a cartridge, then ejects it, the gleaming celebration of brass tumbling to his feet. He has never shot anyone.

Before him on love's scorched plain, the wreck of so much gasping and burning, the long black legs of smoke pacing the horizon. Whole armies march to their deaths before his eyes. How eagerly they bury themselves in the sweeping shadows that cling to the dunes. Days later there's not a footstep left to follow. That's love, always demanding new heroes. A veteran now, love works over time telling him the wounds aren't deep enough, only his death can love him completely.

Geneva Conventions on War

In the shower the water stops falling. The last drops submissively swirl in the drain as the pipes in the wall continue to hiss. The tiles glisten as if Jonah were walking naked along a wet, abandoned cobbled street. All the storefronts have rusty iron bars pulled across their windows and doors. Fog forms glowing cones under lampposts, even after the buildings disappear, and as far as he can see, until there are just shimmering pinpricks. He could be walking into sky, if he can make it that far. He feels chilled. He wants to wrap his arms around himself. There are no alleys to turn down and he can't turn back.

What begins to flow from the shower spigot, fast as water, is hair. Unbroken strands softly run down the back of his head and over his shoulders. Thick coils spin around his legs. His waist is cinched in a fine brown braid. He's back walking the street trailing an elegant mane that touches the pavement. He begins to weep, his tears turn to thatch, his cheeks, the roof of a face he can no longer enter.

Baltic Days

Being Its Time

In a small Baltic town, on a cold overcast day that could have been yesterday a century ago, and for all practical possibilities will probably be tomorrow a century from now, and whose indeterminancy turned the maypole in the hay-stacked field just east of the last half-timbered houses into a spear stuck in the frozen ground by a falling warrior of Valhalla—here Heidegger slipped beyond his and anyone else's journal. He abandoned future biographers who might scour the town for street corners where the great thinker stood, so they could ponder what he might have pondered, such as seeing his reflection in the window of the shoe-repair shop. He stepped away from the preponderance of philosophers who would keep turning the pages until they were blank as the coming Arctic snow. It was there at the small desk in the inadequately heated third-floor room, which was really an attic he rented under an alias, where each breath hinted of the last, that he first wrote that *the only thing worth thinking is the unthinkable.*

Heidegger had dipped his stork-white quill into the inkwell and flown into the dark, not knowing if he would ever return. There was elation among those who thought he had given birth to the unknown or, less, that he made the improbable probable. Accident became coincidence, coincidence synchronicity, and synchronicity the fine-tuning of the cosmos. Whole tired towns swore off potatoes and turnips, and starved, believing they could live on the light of his thinking. These emaciated towns became known as the first voluntary pogroms. A man bloodied his face trying to run through a wall, but the rumor persisted of his success. Throughout the country large bandages flowered over noses, as if an early sign of spring. Women hanged themselves from ceilings, hoping to get closer to heaven, and had to be cut down. Finely braided rope burns around delicate necks became high fashion. Photographers began keeping records of the soul using glass negatives. To be crowned unthinkable became the rage.

For others the century was a curse. There was the unthinkable factory job, the unthinkable war that led to the next unthinkable war, and the unthinkably cold tenements in the cities. The unthinkable kept looming larger, leading to the unthinkable bomb. And then there's the unthinkable God enslaved to eternity, and Heidegger's own unthinkable being thinking in a darkening world.

The Black and Blue Book

In a small unnamed Baltic town, close enough to the sea that one can smell the salt crystallizing in the tidal winds sighing inland each day during the summer months, there was to be found—taking a deep breath that expands the chest into a false sense of belonging to something eternal—a true hint of something beginning. This is when, after a vigorous walk, Wittgenstein—standing at the edge of a green field with his jacket and vest unbuttoned to take in a full measure of this sea-sailed air— admired the maypole still adorned with wilting garlands, and recognized in their flutter that each proposition capable of being true must also be capable of being false. He turned and walked back to town.

On the crowded walls of his small room hung souls frowning with the look of those drowning in deep thoughts. He sat troubled. If in the beginning was the Word—a clearly spoken, though assuredly and not easily understood one— then innocence never existed, since every true word is married to its false complement. So, if in the beginning was the Word, then, also, in the beginning was not the Word. As soon as something was heard, it was not heard. So those rowdy towheaded kids, running up and down the halls, deserved to be slapped and not slapped for not hearing what was not said, or for hearing or not hearing what was said. They weren't supposed to be listening outside the kitchen door to adult whispers about so-and-so being pregnant, or who's drunk. Then again, the kids already knew.

Then there was a creation and there was not a creation—a strange animal eating its tail and turning itself inside out as quickly as it appears. The black hole located under creation's wagging tail wouldn't be discovered until decades later when time and space hit the fan and shredded into sour cabbage. Wittgenstein was becoming agitated. He blamed it on the wood-caned chair that forced him to sit too upright.

Maybe he should take another walk, this time following the long road that leads to the sea—farther than he wanted to go, but perhaps he could obtain a carriage and forget the built-in obsolescence of all creation. Maybe the sea wrack ground fine in ceaseless waves, the gulls picking up the washed up and abandoned, the mysterious creatures crawling back under the wind-ridden water, and the ever-towering cumulus, might not ravel so easily. Maybe he should pack and return to Cambridge, to a schedule of classes. This is not the first time his vacation had become too ponderously cluttered for him to stay the full time in this town. Then he decides to call it a dream, but that does not change anything. In the beginning there were fewer words, that's all, but they hurt just as much, so he turns and walks back into the closet.

Twilight of the Dogs

On a park bench in the flower- and tree-lined square, a retired fisherman leaned back deeper into the afternoon light breaking over the roofs of the nearby shoe and butcher shops and the many *rathskellars*. Late in summer, the sun is always low on the horizon in a town this far north, a town known for the quality of its shoes, sausage, and plentiful drinking. There were beer mugs in the shape and size of boots emptied each day in these basement pubs, and when done the drinker felt he'd walked halfway across this small lowland country and still hadn't reached the door.

The retired fisherman was not one of them. He had moved away from the sea and settled in this quaint inland town, more quaint than his village that was once daily dressed in the intricate weave of drying nets, filled with odors of fresh and decaying fish, its streets glittering with their scales, as if paved with coins that somehow always left it poorer. On the inland side of the village, mounted on stakes that stood like black maypoles, were the skulls of fish hauled out of the stormy sea, their slack-jawed gaping a celebration of the fish-ermen's prowess and bravery, to have defied, to have captured these finned demons. He'd walked the shore, these wet glittering plains, most of his life, now he wanted to be grounded, to stand on hard-packed, cobbled earth.

This town was his savior, his escape from a coastline that shifted with each raging season. Each afternoon for the past week the same stranger had come to sit with him and he listened to this man's odd declarations, his peculiar rantings. Today it was a joke: What does a dyslexic, agnostic insomniac do in the middle of the night? The fisherman couldn't think of an answer, there were no punchlines to years of dragging nets until his hands cramped in the shape of claws. Nietzsche waded through the fisherman's silence, then gave him the answer: He worries about whether there is a dog or not. He began to laugh at his own joke until his sides hurt. He began to sound as if he were barking.

In one of those odd events that can make one believe in

a God, or at least believe the gears of the universe sometimes mesh and are not always stripping the flesh from one's bone, though in this case there was something of both, a mongrel dog raced across the too-green grass and sunk its teeth with a snarl into Nietzsche's right calf. For a moment, he was too stunned to move. After all, Nietzsche had proclaimed God dead, but he hadn't included the obvious antithesis.

To live one's life dangerously, to be an Übermensch, shouldn't mean to be reduced to kicking the shit out of a dog, so he sat there without making a sound or gesture, waiting for the mutt to tire. The shocked fisherman, misinterpreted Nietzsche's inaction as weakness, at best paraylsis, and himself being a man who had pulled barbed hooks from his own flesh and saved companions washed overboard, stood up and booted the dog so hard it rolled to the other side of a nearby tulip bed. It ran away yelping, its skinny tail between its skinny legs. It was here in this small Baltic town that Nietzsche contracted a rabid, infectious embarrassment and became philosophy's biggest joke. A search was made for the mongrel dog. The only proof the jagged scars in his leg.

The Unnatural Daughter

The angled ceilings of the attic room were pinched by the slope of the roof. Standing anywhere but in the center meant perpetually bending over, as if age were a permanent part of being there, at least until the renovation was completed. The townspeople shuddered in their kitchens waiting for the latest metaphysical dislocation to descend upon them with the intensity of a winter white-out from what they called "The Philosopher's Room." There would be days of dementia when a visitor to town would be frightened by the spectacle of people aimlessly wandering the cobbled streets. They would grope along stone walls, their fingers following the crumbling mortar, as if it were the only map that would lead them back to their steaming turnip soup. Soon the skyline was dominated by what was called the "Philosopher's Castle," a turret, and the town was momentarily righted, ruled by incognito kings of thought.

One night Goethe dreamed his last words were "More light. More light." Or was that someone else's death? There seemed to be so many lately and he had begun to confuse others with his own. In the morning he sat at his square desk shoved against the round wall of the turret. He heard soft footsteps coming up the wooden stairs. It was the innkeeper's daughter. She shyly approached him with one of her school assignments. She had written a biography of an actress who performed in the local theater. The travelling troupe, the Danzig Players, had performed The *Lover's Caprice*, an early youthful play of his. They had quickly moved on after a week of poor attendance. She timidly handed him her report and explained that now she must compose a poem, and she didn't know how to even begin. Goethe set the report in his lap and began to read. He was not looking for the daily statistics but for where fact rose up to fiction, and fiction became the shadow of poetry. He wasn't sure he would find it, and surely the innkeeper's daughter didn't know such a place existed in what she'd written. But there it was, a couple of lines that set Goethe's quill to paper, and from those lines he transformed a claustrophobic attic into the heights of a turret. She quietly watched as he reread the poem once, and satisfied, handed it to her unsigned. She thanked him and returned to the kitchen table covered with skinny potato peels and rewrote the poem signing her own name.

He didn't think anything more of it until a few days later when the innkeeper's daughter skipped into the room to tell him that her teacher had proclaimed it the best poem she'd ever received from a student. Her instructor was going to submit it to the Baltic International Literary Contest. It was then that he understood how in this most innocent of acts, their destinies had become inextricably intertwined. In rewriting the poem, she had forgotten a comma and inadvertently changed a verb tense, which moved his poem from his past and into her future. No one would ever be able to separate their words and say this is hers, this is his, and yet she had left him behind, turning him into a historical figure sitting in the park feeding pigeons. Yes, he knew the historical necessity of the apprentice stealing even the light he dreamed.

Either/And

It was in the cafe just off the town square where a decrepit
Hegel, entering for his daily lager, accidentally met the young
Kierkegaard sitting at a table by the window, and was offered
a seat. Hegel hooked his gnarled cane, carved from a blue
ash's branch, over the chair's back. From their corner it was
possible to catch a glimpse of the manicured town gardens
and the tulips with their thick comical buds nodding in the
April breeze, as if unanimously agreeing to another windy
conclusion. They had not yet opened their petals, their plush
rebuttals to the great pessimists, which these northern climes
produce in abundance. Hegel saw these flowers more as
swings of a hammer; if luck held (though he'd say luck was
another name for the great dialectic), his thumb would be out
of the way on the downswing of tulips into their withering
colors, and he wouldn't have to dig any up in his garden.

His young friend is practicing the dialectic of pick-
ing up a frothy stein, bringing it to his lips, setting it back on
the table covered with the initials of many jilted centuries.
Kierkegaard is here to forget a woman, and he tells Hegel it's
not as easy as it looks, giving up her curvaceous lines for erotic
lines of prose. He's already drunk too much and is ready to
argue with the old man that truth is not always whole but
comes in pieces, and right now all Kierkegaard has is pieces.
And furthermore, he says, there's no life in universals, there's
only life in this beer stein shaped like a boot that kicks him
in the mouth each time he takes a drink, and is almost empty
because *he* emptied it—not some universal angst that has no
teeth to lose.

Yes, he salutes Hegel with the dialectic of beer mugs,
full and empty, and its driveling deliriums. He wants to know
where is his heart that he so chooses a blank page over the
breasts of a woman. Hegel listens. He knows. The sun is be-
ginning to throw the peaked shadows of roofs onto the street.
A few tulips did open that day. The men walk out of the cafe

arm in arm, singing beer-drinking songs from their student days, their heads pounding like tubas. Kierkegaard steps into the loss of another sunset. Hegel steps into the glow of all sunsets. Wandering and weaving to the edge of town, one of them sees the maypole falling from ice damage, the other sees the new maypole being raised.

Macchiato

Out the window so much had changed. Dark sinews of stains run down the stone faces of the church across the street, looking as if it were straining to remain standing after all these years, as if it might collapse into its own grief and suffering. Along the parapets, weather had softened the grimace of gargoyles, so now they crouched only in the sadness of northern rains. The massive wooden doors, carved with scenes of holy torment, were deeply fissured, letting seams of light and frigid winds enter freely.

The rutted dirt streets were now covered with cobbles. There were many more houses. The horse-drawn coach that passed him earlier as he walked from the cemetery was elegant beyond his words. He felt awkward, his patience for resurrection had run out. He sat surprised and embarrassed, dusting dirt out of his ancient tunic as he waited for coffee. Clumsy too—his inert hands lie on the table as if they didn't belong to him after so many centuries. His tangled fingers were heaped on the initial-scratched table like yarn teased by a cat, a kabalist's perfect logic that had succumbed to a fact, a fact that was surrounded by the claws of conclusions in an argument that begins to tear itself apart as potatoes in the fire explode.

The table became cluttered with childhood memories. No one in the café noticed when he removed his hand and shook it like a handkerchief, hoping that would straighten his joints. It started as a nervous, childhood game that he remembered as he spooned a parsley-sprinkled turnip soup and sat in front of the frost-wreathed window. He saw himself sitting in the mouth of an illuminated cave where his flock had gathered. Antlered men chanted to call back the sun that was falling off their edge of earth. It was at the table, in this ritual revelry, that he intertwined his fingers and brought his palms together to pray. His thumbs touching, he raised both index fingers, so they formed a hollow upturned "V." He began to recite, "Here's the church," looking at his fists; "Here's the steeple," his index fingers pointing out the window; "Open the door," and he moved his thumbs to look in; and "Here's all the people." It was then he opened his palms and there were no wriggling fingers, no people. He'd done it wrong.

He'd left the people on the roof. That's where they belonged, he decided, gathered on the slate shingles, cavorting with clouds. He proclaimed the floors of his church to be feathers, the stained glass to be bright as parrots, the walls hovering, the wings on the uncrossed altar. He was ready to shepherd this new flock south to the holy warmth, but first he needs a touch of milk in his espresso, a touch of light from the window, a touch of angel for Meister Eckhardt to rise again. After all, his childhood was buried centuries ago.

Night Elegies

Invisible as a crane's head calculating on its fully extended neck above the cattails that blanket the estuary; that's how he watches from the boat of sleep, and then his arm rises and crosses his bedded body for the edge of the nightstand where the clock is rattling apart, where a catcher's mitt-sized clam-shell fields the hardball dark (and this is not even a dream of emigrating to America but of swimming the North Sea), where a quartz crystal refracts a facet of the lamp and throws a tiny window of light onto the wall so the passing clouds are grainy as wood, where an Oriental fan sits with its courtesans and mountains crimped closed but the silk rustle of their kimonos can still be heard above the folded water. This is where his hand finds the earrings, deftly as the crane's bill spears the darting fish.

He runs the small glass beads and thin piping slowly through his fingers. He tries to imagine their shape. Which one did he grab first this morning? Soon he knows. Another night to abandon; his angels did come to roost. Sitting on the edge of the feather bed, he pulls on his earlobe, stretches the single hole until it is an oblong vowel, and then he easily slips the point of the hook through the tongue of air. It is the ear-ring man with the crooked penis that will carry on a day-long monologue, pointing this way and that, never stopping to consider the consequences, making angelic promises, mo-ments of ecstasy it can't keep. So he promises himself that tomorrow he will first wear the woman with one leg, the ear-ring pirouetting just above his shoulder. Yes, all day her one leg moving up and down his neck, until the fine, nearly invis-ible hairs are a choker of fire, and he is forced to lean his head back and stare into an unrelenting blaze of sky. This evening, returning from watching the reconstruction of the maypole at the edge of town, he writes:

> *Is it any less difficult for lovers?*
> *But they keep on using each other*
> *to hide their own fate.*

The wood burning in the fireplace flickers his shadow across the wall. He slips under the comforter; his ears are ringing. In one he listens to Marie, and in the other Rainer, as Rilke tosses restlessly between.

The Unseasonal Town

The town is haunted by more than its doors closed by long
winters and visions that crawl the walls looking for cracks;
the empty streets covered by the seamless page of snow that
descends deeper than the bony burgher's knees, that erases
the horizon and draws the whiteness out of their breathless
bodies; the sky reduced again and again to the next storm,
where the house corners growl with wind, and the only unsafe
conversation is the weather that kills.

The town is haunted by its maypole and rebuilding it
each April, by the green resurgence that is a reminder of every-
thing it wasn't and everything that it can't be, by the growing
stains that darken its stone houses, the desolate earth that
grows rich on its decay, tulips that swear their colors in flower
boxes and along streets, the future that will twist every attic
thought and inflate turrets of reasons into a skyline.

The town is haunted by a distant sea whose salty ru-
mors are carried by wind, that sometimes leaves the feathered
wreck of a strange bird on a doorstep, that fills the old men
in the square by the brass cannon surrendering to tulips, that
sends old women back into their houses to lock the young
behind doors, close windows on hot nights, so the dreams of a
sweaty sea can't enter their lives and wash anymore away.

The town is haunted by all the photographs empty of
a single boarding house or spired church, the maps that show
roads passing and intersecting at nameless doubts, the leafless
trees planted in rows, the fields plowed seasonally by wars,
all the stones that belong to names, even the small flat ones on
unpaved road, that one evening a boy, who plays hooky from
school and on his way home, picks up and skips across the
lake that is only beginning to freeze, the stone skimming and
spinning until the last moment when it sinks, pulling down
dusk.

Captive Flights

Delphic Chicken

"Crito, I owe a cock to Asclepius; will you remember to pay the debt?"
—Socrates after his hemlock

What about Socrates' chicken? After he left the sobbing cell, Crito found Asclepius in a local brew-pub, stumbling through waves of fermented barley. Crito, disgusted with such a public display of grief, not realizing that with each drained tankard Asclepius was being washed farther up on the shore of knowing himself as a pounding headache, walked out and left the debt unpaid. Did Crito then set Socrates' chicken free, leaving Socrates to be known as a legendary bad credit risk; leaving the rest of us with the debt that can never be paid, *gnothi seauton*?

And what kind of life did a destitute chicken live, having lost its master, who was also its slave, feeding and watering it every day, eyeing its plumpness, feeling its firmness, waiting for that ravenous philosophical hunger that wrings hands and necks. There is no getting up from the chopping block. Could it have wandered the alleys of Athens, followed by reverent whispers, "There goes Socrates' chicken"; followed by those people down on their luck, who had made ill-considered investments in goats or been cuckolded for the dozenth time. Did they approach the clucking myth, believing the wisdom of a chicken could stop the widening cracks in their Humpty-Dumpty lives?

Holding out their hands, they delved the gallusic signs: If the chicken pecked too hard and drew blood, that meant no, unless the trickle flooded the lifelines across their palms, which meant the tragedy of their lives would reach historic proportions, and a footnote would be reserved for them, thereby transforming the near- to farsighted and far- to nearsighted in their quest to join the immortal gods; or even better, if the chicken ate the bloodied grain from their open hands, then yes, they should try again to salvage their marriage or underwrite another ship of oil-filled amphoras from Ephesus. In Delphi the capitals at the tops of marble columns are scrolled chicken feathers.

The Rising Flocks

Beside the empty plates the folded wings of angels. The scepters of knife, fork, and spoon sit on the table. The diner's etiquette calls for feathers to be dabbed at the corners of mouths. Lipstick and gravy trace the zenith of their flights. Their wings fluttering across laps are the zeitgeist of arousal, and reason enough for these cravings. A few guests still don't understand and become uneasy when a hand reaches under the table to caress their angelic longings. The tablecloth, rich with spilled burgundy, traces the borders of intoxicated continents that wait to be explored by a pair of fallen tongues, and later with the soft panting of wings. Then there are the insulated angels that can hold up the heated corners of hell and a flaming fondue. For the moment, they keep vigil by the oven door, ready to escort a roasted soul to the carving block.

In the living room the crowd is growing anxious; between the sofa and the ceiling Saint Albert tallies four hundred million of the wingéd, and the kabalists holding up zircon crystals agree. One wet white blur is working through the four thousand nine hundred ninety-nine names of God. Another is half fire, half ice. The spooked guests begin to think angels everywhere, even sending a mission to convert the kitchen witch. And so, no matter how humble and discrete the conception, because the guests can think of angels at all, that must mean there are angels. Soon they'll debate the details and style of God over another glass of wine.

On the radio by the couch, it's reported that an artillery shell exploded on a table in the crowded market of a besieged city. Sirens sailed loudly through the air for hours. Because men can conceive of death, they have become its overheated engines. In the dining room, no one is listening, as Saint Albert uses the Heimlich maneuver on the host who's choking on a buffalo wing.

Occupations

From this distance it is difficult to be certain. Someone must be out there, on the other side of this city, in one of the many ragged streets bounded by hermetic buildings and mists. Jonah's seen the tentative column of smoke rising above the roofs, a wispy finger pointing nowhere but away, a single unraveling gray hair against the blue-skulled sky. He must keep watch, must stay awake, and he grips tighter, whatever is in his hand that is meant to throw, to hurt, to kill, but then he wakes and stares at the dark ceiling of the bedroom before he draws his arm back and aims at the thickening shadow.

Out the window night softens and the oaks grow back into place along the sidewalk. Jonah feels Jessie's warmth huddled next to him and he moves closer. Under the blankets she is a defined comfort and he knows exactly how he fits along her back—two countries bordered by flesh and red rivers. He also knows not to drape his arm over her shoulder and across her breasts to draw her closer. Lately, they have tried to become less occupied.

Spread over the kitchen table are masses of cardboard wafers cut in the shape of amoebas, sorted into amorphous piles by colors and shadings. Jessie says that's as complete as the picture will ever get, and they proceed no further that evening. But the next day at the far end of the table, the box lid is propped on its side displaying the complete picture, something adored or adorable that they should spend their lives piecing together. As is often the case, it's a gift, something later than an afterthought, when nothing more intriguing turned up, and now unwrapped, there's nothing better to occupy their lives. She finds most of the border and fits the small knobby ends into the knobby holes. Now they know the limits. Jonah finds an eye and begins working on the head. The maddening pieces of nearly identical blue sky take days to complete. The skin that repeats the same pattern of glittering scales is just as difficult. One evening he picks up the last piece. She touches his hand. He knows right where it goes.

The weather is warm and wet and foreign. They are occupied countries, occupied by each other's desires. They dance the borders, and each new lyric is a skirmish. At the checkpoint, passports are examined closely, held up beside their aging faces. Histories are remembered. Incursions into forbidden territories are cause for repeated night-long interrogations. Each piece of luggage is opened and clothes held up to the light—then the strip search. All those years of real and false modesty are now officially on display. The caliber of the guard's eyes target all the secrets they have ever carried across these borders. Before the guards can tell them to dress, that tonight they aren't searching body cavities, they confess to every transgression back to their first meeting, and then back to childhood. The guards shrug and turn away, they have a jigsaw puzzle to finish in the back room.

Other nights, in the blue glare of lights at the checkpoint, rifles remain shouldered, the guards lean against their small shack smoking, and all that's needed is a nod of the head to pass, though there has never been an official surrender, an exchange of prisoners, or an accounting of all that's missing.

Some Good Ideas To Dream

This isn't one. Jessie's sleeping on a new mattress and having trouble adjusting, as if she had entered a federal witness protection program and her new identity doesn't fit anything Jonah knows. When she lies down on the mattress, she's no longer sinking in, submerging, waiting to hit bottom—sleeping is no longer a process of absorption. On the new mattress she's flotsam and jetsam, washing up on the world's shores each night. This morning she recalls the scrotal-drawstringed purse, opened and held upside down, given a little shake so its contents fall freely on the table. Not the glitter of coins but denominations of religions tumble and roll across the heavy wooden table, and are deflected by the surface's deeply carved initials. Christianity wobbles down the groove of a "K" before it falls over. Islam follows an "M" over the edge. Before the coin clangs against the tile floor, it vanishes. From the shiny heap in the middle of the table, she grabs one that won't roll away. It's rectangular, surprisingly heavy, engraved with a winged sun and the profile of a stoic cat. Before she remembers more, the stiff mattress shoves her out of bed. On its high edge, she's forced to sit spine-straight, a soldier at attention, ready to march. Another day when they lie down together, wife and husband, they no longer sag toward each other, their bodies no longer forced to accommodate the changing borders of their sleep, their sad lives on weak springs. Removing the sheets for cleaning no longer reveals the stains of their excesses. They hover like wingless angels, their arguments biblical and dusty.

This probably isn't one either: her desire to dream the thighs that will call the saints down, to have tarot readers rebuild their fallen houses of cards, to have crystal gazers uncover their future spheres, the tea-leaf readers to pour themselves another cup with two teaspoons of sugar, the chicken-entrails forecasters to sew feathers back on the plucked bodies, the bone throwers to mend their skeletons, the casters of cracked turtle shells to dampen their fires, and then finally her chest, rib cage spread wide to release her winged heart just for a sound night's sleep, hoping she can reel it back in the morning.

Rain of Shoes

Bruised sweet-gum leaves cover the sidewalk. Small islands of brown grass fidget in the breeze. Thick stalks of darkness grow out of the ground. From the window Jessie watches the apartment buildings sink into shadow. The cars parked along the curb turn sullen and the upturned trashcans surrender their dented shine. Step by step door stoops descend. She's not convinced of the emergency. The third story sinks below the retreating light. Not a single window is illuminated, as if entire floors have been abandoned.

Inside a pitched panic spreads. Desperate mothers drag their crying children, rush up flights of stairs, cram graffitied elevators for upper floors. Old men grab their photo albums and stamp collections, totter in the wrong direction, never to be seen again. Junkies frantically shoot paths into themselves, so nothing of their lives is left behind on filthy kitchen tables. The universe of corridors and stairwells spirals chaotically. An old woman balances a pot of cabbage soup in her arms as she is swept up.

Back in her room Jessie doesn't hear a word of it. She calmly watches from across the street. The reddening fame of receding light floats each brick in its own royal pool. She half expects entire buildings to swim away–a synchronized event with the smell of chlorine saturating the city, towels waiting for fifty dripping floors to dry off. The judges confer before raising their scorecards. The winners and losers go home with ribbons and skylines. She sits alone in her apartment.

Jessie sees late light's cough syrup consistency as it sticks to the top floors of diseased buildings. If she wasn't sitting in that classic window-womb pose of legs drawn up to chest, chin resting on knees, sipping tea as the shadows continue to percolate, she'd see hysterical crowds backed up on mopped-asphalt roofs—leaky life rafts rocking on the last waves of sunlight. She'd see people standing on capstones, their arms uplifted, their fingers touching the low-angled rays. She'd see men and women fumbling with buttons and zippers, throwing their clothes over the edges of roofs, hoping this will enlighten them enough to float naked over streets flooded with a rain of shoes.

Thick With Rumors

A sudden fear grips the city. It spreads wide as a northerly rattling the last leaves on the wrought-iron trees that divide the stagnant canal from the park. The citizens can hear it knocking on every door and face it on every street. It sits next to them on park benches and moves uncomfortably close. They find it staring at them from full and empty coffee cups. They conclude that there is no escape. Janitors and office workers alike, climb to the roofs of art deco buildings and kiss the griffins goodbye before stepping off parapets. The air is so thick and wild with rumors, they float to the ground, maybe twist an ankle when they land. They stand in the middle of streets embarrassed, confused, weeping, dejected, blocking traffic that was rushing to career off piers and bridges. For many weeks men and women hobble on crutches or limp along sidewalks. The entire city rises and falls with each of their steps. A steady seismic activity is recorded at stations around the world. Loose windowpanes never stop shivering.

Those few who resort to more extreme means find razor blades rust instantly in their blood, dulled beyond slashing. The hopeless walk around with Band-Aids covering up the nicks on their wrists and necks. The warm water in bathroom sinks and public restrooms grows coldly red. Drugstores sell out in the first hours of panic. Passing pedestrians begin laughing at each other, seeing the flowered, the rainbowed, the Barbie- and dinosaur-shaped Band-Aids plastered over each other's bodies. Band-Aids become stripes of rank, badges of honor, boring failures.

The city is crowded with pawnshops. Behind their barred windows, the heavier calibers and automatics invite the desperate. Cold steel becomes the demise of choice. Berettas and Uzis begin erupting randomly across the city, the fire-works of anticipation, a celebration of liberation. For those who set the barrel against their temples, the bullets dissolve in a prayer-shawl of smoke, leaving a large number of the citizenry half deaf, regretting their bad aims, and shouting "What?" when asked about the odd powder burn patterns. The citizenry become known for their rhythmic hand dialect.

For those who stick the barrel in their mouths, they simply swallow more air than ever before, forcing more oxygen than usual into their occluded brains, producing days of insomnia, eruptions of lost memories, bouts of uncontrollable clarity.

It's the sight of Band-Aids that finally brings everyone to their senses. These stupid little adhesives around the corners of burned mouths and eyebrows, covering throats and wrists, that touches them deeply, that tells them how even a sprawling congested city, cramped with attempted accidents and failed suicides, could be held together by its wounds.

Avian Cuisine

From the sidewalk tables, the small group of diners turn their heads to watch the gathering flurry of black sparks above the roof of an office building. A car passes unnoticed. They have stopped eating, their forks sit half-buried in dishes of paella. The liquid lenses of their half-filled glasses of rosé invert their upturned heads so they stare down from many private skies into slightly stained horizons of checkered tablecloths. The sky that pours in from both ends of the street and down the sides of the surrounding brick buildings is deeply fermented and fading into streaks of gray. It is an evening when each breath fondly calls forth another, when Jonah across the table can easily pretend to forget his diagnosis and Jessie can forget her junkie son lost somewhere in this city. They will try not to stare over their shoulders through the restaurant window at the television mounted above the bar. There a matador dances around a charging bull until he is flung by its horns, but recovers to bury the sword up to its hilt between the bull's shoulders. The animal stumbles, steps back, falls to its knees, stands once more dumbfounded, then collapses into a black heap of hide and cooling flesh.

The diners are first attracted by the choppy echoing chatter tumbling off the walls along the street. It comes from a whirlwind of eddying swifts descending on the massive chimney of the turn of the century building. Dazzling, uncountable, and at frightening speeds, they enter the charred vertical tunnel, and with a last moment breaking flutter, they disappear. As if the chimney were recalling coals from every fire that had scorched its throat, or was reinhaling the smoky souls released by every long-ago flame, the downturning feathered funnel swirls inward. Hurtling winged embers, there are so many of them, the diners worry and are prepared to duck. With wineglasses in hand, they look into the few lit windows to see if there are birds flying through the offices and down the halls. Each night the birds arrive and sit at desks to carry on the wingless work. Each bird a finger, their wings the curve of eyebrows, their sweeping flights the sum of day. A janitor appears at an alley door, emptying trash. It's the ashes of exhausted flights that he sweeps up from below the windowsills.

This is his nightly routine. He doesn't look up to see what the diners see above him, the building stretching on its foundation to inhale the last swift in the last shimmer of light. The small group quietly gasps swallowing the sharp silence. They feel a fluttering in their chests as they remove the napkins from their laps, politely wipe their mouths, ask for the check, and carrying their purses and jackets, fly slowly down the street.

Shadows of Troy

South By Southwest

1
As you've wasted your life here, in this small corner,
you've destroyed it everywhere else in the world.
                          –C. P. Cavafy

2
So long as I've got one jar of olive oil to put after another
in my brain, I don't have to look at Eternity.
                          –Alan McNary

3
A loose timber from the sun's sunken wreckage floated up
and was dawn on the water.
                          –Mark Richard

Born Under Glass

For always in time past the gods
have shown themselves clearly to us . . .
—Odyssey

Book 1

The Greeks, catching their citizens' comings and goings, buried
their dead next to the roads that led into towns, and some-
times away. Romans followed in their footsteps not knowing
what else to do. Changing the names of gods didn't protect
the innocent in the far barbaric provinces. The plaque on the
wall doesn't explain all of this to him, so in front of the diorama
he begins to search where the green-sprinkled Styrofoam grass
stops and turns into a painted scene.

The road wanders off into what must really have been
overgrazed hills, though they are gently rolling and the flame
of distant poplars flickers at the bottom of a cirrus-swept
sky—the artist's favorite weather for eternity? The road is a
limp, gray meander where it crests the last silhouetted ridge.
Only the barefoot could have followed it, and now nothing
returns after these many centuries except broken bones.

Against the glass there are the nameless graves, small
holes cut into the Styrofoam with a razor blade, and for au-
thenticity, the ashes of a dog fired at a local veterinary clinic
scattered in one of the open holes. He sees that it is modeled
after a woman's burial; doll-sized bracelets and an ornate
jewelry box lies beside an intricately decorated urn.

The next grave is that of a warrior and the urn is also
unbroken, sealed under a stone untouched by robbers or
archeologists and the illusion of time. There is a "killed"
sword the size of a toothpick wrapped round the urn. He
reads that this bending was a show of respect, telling others no
one else could use the blade as bravely. Miniature spearheads
sprout in the facsimile earth at the urn's circular base.

The thumb-sized pottery was hand painted under a mag-
nifying glass, as if excruciating details were our only certainties.
There are more small holes, shrinking a millennium of death

rituals to fit the glass case, ending with the shroud-inhumed. He wants death to stay this small, so it will fit into a breast pocket, and when he bends to look closer or tie his shoe it will topple out onto the carpet, and someone else will pick it up, believing it lost, and carry it home.

Book 2

The real artifacts reside in other displays along the hall. Most of what's left is what the dead took with them, then dropped and couldn't pick up again: small horn-snouted bronze horses and ceramic votive trays, beads and a silver bird pendant, spectacle-shaped dress pin and pomegranate vase for rebirth, painted tankards and pyxis. Their painted scenes depicted in profile, as if no one planned to face down three thousand years, and now they are giving up, fading away. In earth tones the human torso is always an inverted triangle, the heroically nude remain exposed, Helen's abduction by Paris doesn't stop, the sacred marriage of Zeus and Hera is preserved. The clay cracks and is glued together, and cracks again.

In front of each display he sees his reflection, how it has a certain barbaric appeal. Soon he's no longer looking at the oil flask from Cumae or the monumental krater from Athens. Amid the shards of all these stories, his reflection hovers on the pottery's curvature, on the wasp-waisted lions and harlequin-suited beasts. The clay owl with breasts flaps against the back of his eyes. He is the finger-high statue with a cribbage-peg erection. He's there in the Submycenaean, slipping deeper into its clear void, a history that suits his every move.

He panics as his lungs crystallize. He shouts, but what survives is the silence of museums, not the assembled debris. Then once inside the glass he calms to a cool thin joy, watching a trunk with two arms, two legs, crude as these clay fragments, turn and walk stiffly to the next display case. There's nothing left to excavate. He becomes an ancient mourner hired to clean the pane, to wipe away the accumulated dirt of seeing. He doesn't follow the faceless groping into the Egyptian room and beyond.

Odysseus in Springfield

Book 3

It's almost winter when he arrives and the city's name hasn't yet changed. He ascends to the fifth floor in a spiral tower of wandering souls. From his balcony he listens to a piano sonata, one he doesn't recognize, which has its emotional moments, but will not escape the dark where it lyrically floats, and never survive beyond this evening. He doesn't know that he will survive this night to hear the same piano played with a shovel.

Unlocking the door to his room, he refuses to rush directly to the couch and search behind it for his death. He knows this is a mistake, there are so many eager accomplices, but what would he do if he found one smiling? Uncap the point of his pen and threaten a revision? One mistake confounds another, and this time his death is asleep under the bed that he has thrown himself on top of, his naked arms and legs stretched toward the corners of the mattress, as if he were embracing the kingdom to come, and not simply embarrassingly close to being buried by the swirling arpeggios of music mixed with voices coming from the other side of the door.

A sea of voices, and though there are distinct words, he doesn't understand. He can hear wind whistling between the sea's teeth. He hears knocking as if half-submerged logs were banging slowly against the hulls of a sunken fleet. Perhaps not laughter, but a flock of raucous gulls on their way down the hall or to the next room. He hears the sighing tide of a door open and spread over a beach dressing itself in evening mist. He hears a door slamming as the surf pounds on a rocky coast.

Later, as the tower is drained of souls and the silence broods, he recognizes the city as it hums a single monotonous note—a Siren's song that scorches the streets, and without his hands and feet bound to a mast he's drawn to its solitary edge. He closes the door behind him.

Book 4

It's late afternoon when he crosses to the bus station, incon-
spicuous except for the emaciated gray dog painted on a rusty
metal sign. Inside he realizes there is no schedule he can
keep. He can't predict how shipwrecked his life will become.
Holding a telephone book, he pretends he is a seer. Nearby,
the empty sleeve of a gray-haired man swings freely as he
picks up pennies thrown by children. His missing hand is
full and pennies begin to slip between his missing fingers. A
small crowd of adults silently applaud, nodding their heads
in unison. He has stopped turning pages and stares at a tall
stoop-shouldered man who has pulled his greasy baseball cap
down tight on his forehead, leaving his face completely lost
in a tangle of beard. When the old man turns toward the late
sun streaming through the dirty window, there's a burning
bush mounted on a skinny neck from which the lost com-
mandments are muttered. Bulging women hug the walls, their
bodies threatening to escape from every seam in their clothing,
and those not already worn out are wearing out faster than
they can leave the terminal. Parents are queued for tickets,
in a hurry to make sure their child won't miss the next sched-
uled departure of the missing. The bus arrives late, the driver
is last to disembark. He limps through the glass doors. The
whole building rises and falls with each of his lame steps.

Book 5

Dazed, he drops the telephone book that he's held all this
time and staggers into the parking lot toward the city's failing
heart. The first two blocks are abandoned. On both sides of
the street the storefront windows are nearly opaque with dust.
In another couple of years the excavations can begin, but what
can be learned that won't be lost or sold again? There are no
signs of life, except for a single surviving specialty business—
six-foot-high Barbie in a polka-dotted swimsuit painted on
the glass and the unopened boxes of Barbies for all occasions
stacked inside, but even its door is locked. In the next block is
the manicured Shriner's temple, its two onion domes crowned
with brass crescents that glow in the sun. There are two small
patches of grass surrounded by sidewalk on either side of the

long canopied entrance. The foundation block reads 1922. The intricate glazed tile facade, color of the desert, blows up and down the street. He coughs in the sandy exhaust of a passing bus. There's a long sweep of burgundy glowing on the bottom of sky when he escapes back to the tower of wandering souls.

Lost Crew

Book 6

. . . the victim and the executioner.
                    –Baudelaire

The snow begins to melt, and the yellowed grass spikes up from a poorly seeded lawn left half-finished by a construction crew. He sits in a parked car thinking it looks more like clumps of hair left after chemotherapy or radiation, or whatever it is we choose to do to ourselves after we discover that it's too late, that it's been done to us.

This isn't to blame the victim, we all are victims, and not to diminish the executioners either. They hone blades on their own histories, which is also us. From that first eye-opening moment after birth when our luminous gray irises float on small fat faces, when we see through it all and never see a thing again, when we are nothings with limitations, it's really the world falling in on us.

The random patterns turn our small hairless heads, if we have the strength, and no matter which way we look there is something falling into our nothingness. If we cry, the liquid lenses just magnify and bring whatever it is closer and upside down in the sliding of our salts. We can't stop the faces from falling down on us: mother, father, siblings, all the strangers that we later search for, flipping through photo albums, phone books, skimming rush hour crowds on city streets, for the rest of our and their lives, believing there's a chance we can re-solve, perhaps understand that one haunting glimpse from so long ago.

In jaundiced lighting of airport terminals, slouching in stiff chairs, we exhaust ourselves half-recognizing each traveler who passes, the concourse filling with half-recollections, thinking this is how they might look twenty, thirty years later, leading a child or carrying a briefcase, walking arm-in-arm with someone we should know, smiling, waving goodbye, hello. We must restrain ourselves from running up to them, saying, "Aren't you. . .? Did you know. . .? Do you live in. . .? Did you go to school at. . .?" Restrain ourselves if only to save our reputations and conceal the desperation, knowing we carry this same burden around with us, that we are only half recognizable to anyone else, half of what someone's searching for, yet we will wear out our knees trying to make up the difference with the half of us that hasn't drifted beyond our reach, the half that someone else is sure they know, though we have never met them before.

He sits in a parked car staring at the snow's conflagration, the glare off the remaining sooty patches, and flips through the pages of Homer that he has promised himself to read. He catches a movement out the corner of his eye, and wonders if it's someone who thinks he knows him. Quickly he turns his head, glances in the rearview mirror, but there's only the smoldering shadow of Troy.

Book 7

It's happened before along the Calypso coast, hitchhiking south from San Francisco thirty years ago, the sound of ocean louder than the traffic on the highway, as if the cars were driving into the sea. In the distance seals raced surfers through the waves, a sea lion barked and begged at the end of a pier, and on the other side of the street someone he'd known from a thousand miles and battles away. They ran across the median laughing and embracing, banging their dented selves together, no longer halves but part of a whole. They turned around and headed north for a few days, then parted, and he never saw him again, but then it seemed so everyday, those journeys, and now he can't even recall a name.

And again, in a Taos grocery store, passing the cereal aisle, he saw the back of another man's head and thought it looked like the poorly lumbered forests around Korinthos long ago. He stopped, returned to position himself to catch a glimpse of the man's face, and it was someone he knew from city-states away. They sacked each other's groceries and drove up into the mountains to the Ponce De Leon Hot Springs, an abandoned resort from the thirties that catered to the rich and the artistic, and from there they watched the sun turn bloody on the slopes of Mount Parnassus and pour into the scar of the Rio Grande Gorge that stretched across the Plains of Marathon. Thousands of feet below them the darkness deepened into a wide crack, and they floated above it, in the steaming water rising out of the earth, their souls dissolving. The next day the man traveled west and he returned to the Midwest. Nine months later, returning from the Ionian Coast, outside Indianapolis, half asleep, wanting to share the driving, he slowed to pick up a hitchhiker and stopped in front of a badly lumbered forest.

Book 8

He's still sitting in Ithaca's parking lot catching the glint and shadow of something, as if someone were ducking behind the car, but again there's nothing, just this diseased grass and aging snow. Nothing, no one struggling for a goodbye, a hello, no dog gasping its last heartfelt breath. He looks back to the book in his lap, turns the page, and sees the sun flash off the paper, reflect in the windshield, and he dives across the seat, dodging the blade of light.

Odysseus Exits KC

Book 9

Cruising at 35,000 feet, he has a window seat. Where his feet
rest is soft and wet, his coat recovering from a snowstorm.
He leans over and begins digging through the pockets for his
ticket and finds old watches, their wristbands knotted together
and slippery as a nest of snakes. None of the watches have
stopped, their small arms continuing to circle their tattooed
faces, at times marking a moment when they half expect their
owners to return, though he knows they are all falling out of
time and this noon sky.

Snakes writhe in his grip, keeping time with flick-
ing tongues. The woman in the next seat, hair in serpentine
braids, confesses the imperfections of her perfect life, and
shivers at the hiss of the overhead air vents. It's the constant
cavernous rush of engines filling the cabin that lulls her and
the other passengers into time's sleepy coil.

It was there earlier, before takeoff, as everyone watched
from their high-backed seats, making sure not to miss an in-
flection of the flight attendant's movement as she followed the
intercom's explanations, her manicured hands pointing out the
exit signs, the exit chutes, the trail of lights down the aisle floor
leading to the exit doors, the floatable seat cushions, the clear
plastic breathing masks that fall automatically if the cabin
depressurizes, the silver seat buckle that she tightens around
a nonexistent waist until even nonexistence is threatened. He
watched the passengers silently stare into the wrinkled face
framed by platinum blond hair, how they wanted to believe
her every move.

He stares out the triple-paned window at the black-
and-white quilt of farms that they must fall towards. The pilot
announces the flight is being rerouted. There is an unques-
tioned silence that settles in the cabin. The passengers avoid
each other's eyes. They simply tighten their seat belts, ease
their chairs back as far as possible.

Book 10

Suffering jet lag, he can't wait for yesterday's miracles to catch up. His itinerary is set: a wealth of uncertainty, storms of will or lack of it, blunt misunderstandings, and all the accelerations and reaccelerations: reverse thrust, the withdrawing, as if anything can ever be taken back, and every word, every action that floats out beyond this little porthole waiting for someone to explicate it, to steal it from time.

Once again he must falsely deny that he wasn't devoured by soft enfolding lips. The moist highway never went on forever the way he wanted. He's safely back in the air, banking left, right, a winged silver spoon in a seething bowl of winter clouds. He could tumble out with the rest of the passengers and live a clouded life selling cooling towers, Avon, quality management programs, but he's buckled, as gray fissures of evening begin to solidify in the upper world.

There's no escaping the gods of turbulence, no way to elevate above memory's jetsam. Passengers continue to search for a break in the clouds, hoping to see and then seeing the city's glitter sprinkled over the earth. For a moment, he swears an allegiance to each streetlight, to the tiny windows boxing their illuminations, to the red bracelet of taillights slowly coiling itself around the tangle of a wreck, and he's thinking, if he can just make it to Gate 537. There's no one waiting. This is a connecting flight.

Book 11

Another emergency landing, and so what if Hera was witnessed to play with a dog's genitals in her own living room. What's so shocking? He had a friend in elementary school who would peel back the hairy leather sheath with his index finger and thumb, exposing his pet dachshund, standing aside to make sure he didn't get peed on, and now he's a colonel in the army.

Dachau was only thirty kilometers away and the town's name has no other context. Its past is its future. It's just a few kilometers away from all of our beds. Hera slept with the smell every night for years and told herself it was anything but that, and finally she believed her guilt. How much can anyone downwind breathe before a dog's hind end begins to look reasonable, to look good, to feel like something it isn't.

Deplaned, bedded in the City of Brotherly Love, all he has is the dream where he's cut in half. He only exists from the waist up and Hera is there below the dream he can't remember, below the glistening slate that cuts him in half and stretches to the horizon, below where he sits like a vase with two useless arms and his mouth open, below the mineral glare that's too hot to touch, below the sun that burns his chest and threatens to boil his skin, below where even Persephone stands, below the foul-smelling Cerberus, below where she can't be recalled.

Odysseus Skips the Revolution

Book 12

The walls of the colonial house are two feet thick. The Liberty Bell cracked before it ever rang. Frugal Ben Franklin's tombstone is covered with tourists' pennies.

A window sunk far back into a stone and log wall, the deep recess protecting him from the weary columns of fog marching past. The medallion of a spider's abandoned body hangs suspended in one corner between glass and torn screen. Another spider caught in its own fall on a strand of web, legs folded behind its translucent body, is the shape of a tear, as if he was crying spiders as he stares into his own thin reflection.

For a moment, he leaves his hand hanging in front of him, a fingered arachnid. He sits on the edge of a mattress in a room crowded with centuries-old furniture. The headboard touches the ceiling. The dark cornucopia of wood unfurls scrolls, shells, vases, vines. Currents of grain pour from within swirls of grain. There's a heavily framed mirror taller than its reflection and a marble-topped chest of drawers.

He is in the land of revolutions, of cross-creek skirmishes, hilltop battles, and the valley of looming defeat. Here roads are too old to be straightened and wind down into valleys between tall maples, past moss-covered water wheels and stone grist mills, the first continental Catholic Church, and spent graveyards that have forgotten their denominations.

This gray day threatens to dissolve more deeply into mist and take the thick men dressed in camouflage, huddled in the middle of fall fields, assessing their hunted histories, with it. Utopias and nostalgia are simply dependent on the weather, and the forecast is always for a couple of good days, starting tomorrow.

Book 13

Christmas lights from years past braided along the top of the iron railing, sag on hooks between columns along the porch eaves. Red and white, red and white, the bulbs, flaking their tint, alternate like his life: island and sea, crisis and calm, and if they were turned on and flashing, that breathless, confused moment between, is where he sits.

A clay bell hangs at the far end, soundless, no paean to arms, no call to the barricades, no proclamations of resistance or liberty, the day's revolution has diminished to a quiet rain. Protected by the roof, strata of quarry dust from across the road have settled on the painted floor boards and the small circular table that sits alone accompanied by a single chair. His coffee cup sweats, leaves a ring of mud. There are cat's paw prints up the steps and the blank soles of his worn-out shoes. Behind him are windows that remain sealed, curtains always pulled closed, and aphotic rooms, rooms that have grown tired of their long celebrated histories of decline.

The struggle continues, a rearguard action. The children know this, who come up to him and lead him by the hand. They climb the hill behind the house to show him abandoned cisterns, a dump of steel rails and shards of patterned glass, a fallen-in one-room school, a greenhouse lost in wild vines, a boarded-up mansion.

Book 14

At the reception for a thousand-mile death, he recalls, as if it were a thousand years ago, the blue dust of the day filling the sky making it difficult to breathe, forming a lump in his throat that he couldn't swallow. He remembers the long stories of the wind that rushed in through the car window, how it vanquished once more the leaves, throwing them down again behind the car, as it crossed the cemetery.

He stands listening, holding back the taste of bad coffee, as another mother reveals to another son that she knew, and knew years ago, that he had thrown the cat into the swimming pool, and when she returned from shopping, how he panicked, knowing she would be hysterical, and threw the sopping cat in the freezer. Five hours later she opened those white doors and found the cat curled up, frozen stiff, something preserved from the Paleolithic.

Everyone in the circle, holding their finger food and punch, laughed at the man who pointed at his brother. The cat wrapped in towels survived without the tops of its ears and most of its tail, but would never enter a room with a white door. He leaves them in another story and steps outside into the still blue day, the lace of sunlight spreading over the brown lawns, over the earthly paradise, over every revolution conspiring in parking lots.

Keelhauled

Book 15

On the island of "Little Spain," Bartolomé de Las Casas is witness to humans burned *thirteen at a time in memory of Our Redeemer and his twelve apostles*—the slowness of the fire, the dripping fat, its sputtering resurrection in the flames. The butcher shops sold arms and legs, and finer cuts, for dog food. Contests challenged swordsman to halve a living body with one stroke.

Odysseus imagines he's one of the Spanish captains sailing a slave ship, without compass or charts. He follows the trail of floating corpses dumped overboard by the ship ahead, and if there wasn't a bloated body to mark the way, the helmsman looked for thrashing sharks. No, he decides he's not the captain, he's the hull of the caravel, the thick planks of wood bent to fit the curve of the sea and wind, but now the ship sits in a dead calm, under a cloudless sky. There's a slight rocking from the drifting, facedown bodies dragged in the currents, their legs and arms outthrust, as they fall through the sea. The bleached bodies crowd the hull, softly knocking against the wood. The crew, the chained slaves below deck, the captain, are frightened by the spectacle. The drowned lifting the ship onto their shoulders, toss the ship backward, turn it over, and carry it to where the living cannot imagine.

Of his forty years in the Americas, Bartolomé de Las Casas says, *Were I to describe all this no amount of time and paper could encompass this task.*

At the Abyss

Book 16

His eyes fall thousands of feet. He stands on a bouldered ledge feeling safe, not groping through thin air toward an expected demise impaled in a salt bush or pierced by prickly pear pads. Next to him lime-colored lichen clings to a swollen rock. A shaft of sunlight slices through pines at his back. Another stone, the size of a kitchen table, balances over a body-wide crack. The valley bottom is shadowed with blue palo verde and cat-claw acacia. Because he is only human, he notices how the rock next to him once sat like a knot of hair twirled into a bun and then fell; how ridges of granite could be eyebrows separated by a scar, and below the gash are four brown-stained teeth.

The earth opens before him. This is what happens when he sits on the side of a mountain too long: acres of light shift their dusty pastels before the ebb of evening and a rising star-stricken night, the slow waves of mountains crashing down into darkness, the surf of blood rushing his ears. Overhead the glint and distant rattle of jet engine, the bright blade of its contrail slicing the earth's penumbra, as it slips into sky's dark scabbard. From this promontory he watches the fading history of crack and abrasion, the shattered and crumbling, the contusion of time and spiraling of space. He knows that the mesquite roots until it finds water, plumbing mine shafts to 200 feet; that cactus are ribbed to store water and thorned to keep it, a thousand little crosses to ward off the thirsty; that the desert's blue-throated hummingbird's heart thrashes at 1,200 beats per minute, its sleep hibernation, its waking a resurrection; that the creosote bush secretes an oily curse to keep its distance in the world; that as these mountains turn milky, they cradle an abyss sprinkled with a few ranch lights where he is marooned.

The Feast

Giant Dirty Trick

If a table is a door, that would explain why when Jessie lay across its flat swirling grain, she was still standing, and why when Jonah lay on top of her, he felt so awkward, and why his pants fell to the floor as fast as Galileo's cannonball dropped from the leaning tower, and why she had to keep pulling her dress up from around her knees, as if confirming the gravity of this event. The table legs sat unevenly on the floor, bowed from the weight of so much history passing over them. The wooden legs' knocking didn't stop, grew faster and louder until that moment when the explosive longing for forever was over, the conclusion imperfect, and they get up to answer different doors.

If a table is a bridge that crosses two rivers, and on one a flock of swans scar the dark water, hustling for crumbs thrown by the lovers, and on the other an excursion boat maneuvers for a better view of the ramparts blown apart centuries ago, and there Jessie and Jonah sit opposite each other at opposite ends of this massive imponderable wooden surface, behind glasses of water and souvenir salt shakers from different cities, their plates mounded with nothing but the salt of their longing, holding their forks and knives at attention, alert as sentries at the bridgeheads, each waiting for the other to take the first step, then this hunger is not so unexpected.

If a table is only a window without walls, through which Jessie and Jonah are left to stare at each other, one from underneath, the other from above, and at any time they will switch positions, depending upon the dominant mood, it is easy to guess the origin of their obsessive need to wipe every fallen crumb and spaghetti sauce dollop clean, holding a hand cupped at the table's edge to catch and carry what's brushed aside to the sink. After all, they would want to remove all barriers in their eating toward each other. But it's easier to understand the unpaid bills strewn on the table among the day's old newspapers, the growing stacks of half-read magazines and books, the limp hot pad, the backs of envelopes scribbled with messages and quotidian lists, the interminable quotidian lists.

Magic Morning at the Zoo

An overcast morning light softens the window. A cat is perched on the sill in an upright ancient Egyptian pose. It watches the widening circles of rain on the puddled sidewalk as the early monuments of day ripple awake. If a table is a bed, then Jonah's looking for his voice under the pillow floating on a bed of gravy. He can't understand what has happened. It was banging in his head at dinner, issuing from his lungs and throat when he lay down. The room is not that dark. Surely, if he had taken his voice off and thrown it down with his pants and shirt, there beside the bed last night, he could see it lying curled around itself like a still sleeping cat. So what if the pile of clothes looks like a wizened balloon that someone pricked with a pin—if there is something to say, say it.

Jessie is angry as Jonah holds himself up, his arms straight, elbows locked, his palms flat on the mattress on either side of the elegant, diminutive curving of her shoulders. She wants to hear him—emphatic, definitive, curdling the air—she wants a voice that will scorch her, that will crack open the day and let her fall through, and keep falling. She wants to hear how she wrenches loose what's screwed too tight inside him, how he rips his chest open exposing his purist heat. She wants him down on his knees cowering before his own belli-cose yawp and thunder. She wants to stroke his snarl, scratch his growl, then draw back her bloodied hand, unleashing him for a four-legged race across his own fevered plains. But he's afraid of that animal.

All Jonah can offer is the rattle of old bones, the flap of tattered fur skins across the entrance to the tent, the wind winding up into the great unringing bell of the spinning world. Still he strains for the scent of a wild edge: the snap of a winter weed across a field, the fired hiss of wet logs, the col-umn of smoke above the trees at the top of a hill where a body burns. Jessie wants to feel what will shake her apart, but he must enter the cage and tame ancient shames. Looking down at her, in the slow movement that they complete, he can't tell if the scratches on his chest and arms come from inside or from without. The cat still sits quietly on the windowsill. The brown laundry of leaves on the oak continue to twist into winter.

The Missionary's Other Position

If the table were a sidewalk that sloped steeply down into a
park, a pocket of green with a creek, a few scattered trees and
barrier bushes wedged between streets, parking lots, and build-
ings, it was certainly no coincidence, since Jonah wandered past
bookstores and coffee shops, that on this sunny September day,
warming back into summer even as evenings fall forward into
violet skies, that he sits at the base of a sycamore for a lunch
that he didn't bring. He has an hour to plot his escape, which
he rarely does anymore, having reconciled himself to no other
way, but always wondering if he has ever honestly tried. The
leaves are beginning to thin, becoming translucent, reflecting an
ethereal light, and across the grass a Rorschach of shadows stirs
with the slightest breeze. He sees beside him on the ground
messages of loss, domination, of a deepening separation.

Today he sits back leaning against the trunk of a tree
whose leaves are falling like a folding card table. The creek is
the rising accumulation of leaking faucets and storm drains.
His arms extended, balanced on his knees, he holds out before
him a cup of coffee, as he watches the water that has lost all
its playfulness, dragging itself through a maze of broken con-
crete. A woman steps out from behind the peeling trunk and
sits down beside him. For a moment they are silent. He doesn't
even glance her way. They both watch a bicyclist wobble past as
he tries to reclasp a pant cuff to keep it out of the sprocket chain.
Office workers stroll on the sidewalk and across the grass.
There aren't any children.

She turns and says hello. They know each other from
work. She's in wholesale and he works in retail. Without fur-
ther introduction, she begins to describe pulling off her blouse
last night, her hair cascading over her face, the flip of her head
that rippled her hair back, how she reached to unclasp her
bra, how her shoulders thrust forward coyly protective of her
breasts, how she stepped out of her fallen skirt and with her
back turned she stretched, deepening the curve of her spine,
then raising one leg at a time, she slipped out of everything else
she wore. With her hands holding down each of his shoulders
against the mattress and her knees drawn up on either side of

his hips, she began to come down into his body.

The creek, which is a table without legs, carries the small debris of last night's drizzle. A cardboard box has collapsed and half-melted into a dam. A gray pool forms, reflecting the opposite bank. A bloodred bird drops out of the body of the tree and onto the grass near them. The sound of traffic is lost in their concentration. Jonah begins by saying he was already naked when he pulled off her shoes and began massaging her feet, one toe at a time, and then worked his fingers up her calves, and the outside of her thighs, so the tips of his fingers ran along the elastic of her underthings until the silk became moist. When she was completely undressed, she rolled over, her head on the pillow as she pulled her knees underneath her.

The leaf shadows continued their incomprehensible display. Sleeves of light reached down through the branches to the ground. Jonah looks at his watch, it is already one o'clock. He stands, brushes off small pieces of wood mulch sticking to his pants. She stands, watches the park empty and return to work. At five o'clock she will drive south directly to her apartment. He will drive farther south. Later she will fluff the pillow on her bed before lying down. Even later he will reposition the gooseneck lamp and read a book on brachiopods to fall asleep.

Garden of Delights

If a table is a garden, then it will take years for mineral and vegetable to serve and nourish each other. It will be more years before anyone else sits down to feast. And even more years for the patients to recover. But what happens between this waiting?

There are many ponderous horses' flanks that must be stood behind, stables to be raked and shoveled clean, sweat to mix with the stale odors of urine, rotten hay to be bucked and forked out of fields, always wary of the snake coiled underneath, quick to strike the blind groping hand, the ground wasp's nest that will spring alive, the spider racing to escape across the soggy bale and the holey glove, the panicked biting of broken anthills, and the squealing skewered rat wriggling on the pitchfork tine. All for a lifelong promise that something can grow in a small corner of an eroding, overgrazed life, that truckloads of ruined straw and alfalfa, with their exotic cities of fungal growth, collapsing as it is plundered into rusting flatbeds, will nurture the soil.

Along the way, the truck is stuck and unstuck in mudholes and creeks. It is obsessively driven to the garden, to the hard pan that refuses the easy shovel, that carves like wood when the booted blade is driven in, that believes in its inert self more than in root and leaf, and even after seasons of turning under this dank-hauled holocaust, the clay refuses to acknowledge its coming breakdown, but slowly succumbs anyway to burrowing worms and grubs, and years of rest under the thick linen of mulch.

The garden weathers plagues of blister beetles and mustard fleas, sucking the boot of too much rain and cracking the heel of too little. At the table Jessie and Jonah's chairs are pulled back slowly, the invitation decades long. She strokes the minerals in his chest, he kneads the vegetables along her spine. They sit down between rows of marigolds and a river of chrysanthemums, to survive, to eat flowers, to savor the small morsels of evening light.

Unholy Rooms

Shaking Yggdrasil

In a city he has forgotten, Jonah opens his mouth to ask directions and all he hears is rustling, as if a northerly were rushing up and out of his chest, billowing his brown shirt. He shuts up, embarrassed, and quickly starts walking away, living up to his whalular defeat. He retreats to the vegetable kingdom. The street's low brick buildings offer up a hundred doors, and today they are all open, as if the redundant despairs of the uprooted and pruned could no longer contain themselves. On the east side of the street, he realizes there is a tree growing in his throat, an ash whose withered leaves cling to its branches long after the other trees are bare. Before he's finished coughing, there's a grove of windswept trunks shaking his voice.

The rooms on his left are classically empty. The painted light, streaming through their windows and across the floor, is folded up one wall. He smiles. The room across the hall is filled with rotting apples. He claims to have taken the first bite. There's a part of him that wants to accept that nothing more can be done. These rooms are finished, the perfect unin-habitation. Still, his only clue is the boy who sits high in one tree trying to coax a tortoiseshell cat from a still higher branch. In another tree a woman tries to assuage the sky and strokes its blue fur.

Something tickles the back of his throat. A breeze agitates the ash's desiccated leaves. Thousands of papery eyelids begin falling. Soon the tree is blind and begs to know if it is headed in any direction. When asked, he coughs up leaves. In a spasm he doubles over, as if he were hacking up a hair ball. He opens his mouth wide, as if he were lying back in a dentist's chair, squinting in the glare. A bemused voice asks if his jaw is numb; a hand probes with a saw to see if there is any feeling. In his mouth, behind the crooked picket fence of his teeth is a man, both his hands swinging open a gate. In the mouth of this smaller man is a woman in a tree, and so on.

Historica Dentata

It started when Jonah's teeth no longer fit comfortably in his mouth. It was not that they were growing like dandelions on a golf green, or that he had fangs hanging over his lips and down the sides of his jaw, as if he were headed toward extinction with the saber-toothed tiger. One day his teeth were rooted in sand. In the mirror their yellowed enamel reminded him of picket fences around summer beach houses—a gummy placid sea visible between each board obliquely bent under the weight of sailored skies. His mother washed his mouth out with sand. His breath turned salty and smelled of sea wrack: twisted kelp and chipped brachiopods, translucent vertebrae and oil-soaked cormorants, spiny urchins and flaccid squid. His friends thought he was a sea of babbling, that he was backstroking through a riptide of gibberish when asked the simplest question. It was just his tongue trapped and drowning in his mouth's tide pool.

Another day Jonah's teeth are poker chips tossed on the green felt of his gums. All around the table, faces are tense. The edges of brows suffer minor tremors. The bets are in: past lives, a month of Sundays, once in a blue moon, the future tense. The croupier looks into the eyes of the players; they float in a bottomless waiting, the last card about to be turned. When his mouth is shut, his teeth are a sealed deck. The dealer peels back his lips, makes the first cut and shuffles, there's no sense of order left: canines shoving out incisors, molars replacing front teeth, bicuspids ready to fall down his throat. When his finned tongue lunges in and out between his lips, they play "go fish." It's all very confusing to him, sitting on a stool with a mouthful of seawater, little enamel boats moored to his gums clinking together. Holding only a pair of deuces, the sails of his teeth burn and sink toward Valhalla.

But when his teeth began to trumpet, graze from one side of his mouth to the other, and his head shifts under their ponderous weight, Jonah stops standing straight, falls toward one precipice or another, and with a lumbering vertigo sway he walks down the hall. He makes an appointment with a dentist. Hanging on the antiseptic glare, suspended in elevator music gurgling from the ceiling, the dentist smiles and says, "It's your age. Your teeth are beginning to drift." He thinks of Hannibal, forever the showman, how he ordered burning torches tied to the horns of a thousand oxen before stampeding them toward the Roman soldiers trapped in the dark; enough to rattle any pagan's teeth. Even elephants couldn't save him. Publius Scipio pulled all Hannibal's teeth at Zama in Numidia, and sent them as trophies to Rome. Hannibal always wore a ring with a secret chamber for such occasions. He would sail off in a dental chair before being captured alive.

The Sickness of Buildings

Jonah is burning all the blank pages. On the desk in front of him there is already a small fire. He is feeding it faster and faster, single pages and handfuls. The walls waver and bend in the flame's flicker. If it were up to him, there would remain no blank pages anywhere. The grotesqueries: how much has already been said, how far it has gone, how it will all be coming back soon. But what's worse, how much can still be written. An army of words is marching down the hall to his door. He can hear the hard syllables of their boots. He can't remember which side he is on. He swore allegiances; he never swore an allegiance.

He must hurry. Sweat stings his eyes. The room swims in smoke. He is surrounded by the flames of blank pages. He can hear their screams to be saved. They are crying for just one word, just one simple word before they blacken and become indistinguishable from the day's declining ashes. To leave no trail and escape through the window, he must walk the ceiling. But he can't do it, he can't chance even the simplest, straightforward request. He's been deceived before.

He knows how one word leads to another. How they are inextricably connected. One word can't leave the next alone. It's contagious as tuberculosis. Then there's all that doubling back and hiding between, and soon it's two o'clock in the morning, the air chilly on the porch and there's nothing that he can say to get himself out of this.

Jessie's sitting by the bed, he's still talking, and there's not one word that can save him. Now her clothes are off and he's still talking. The pages inside him are screaming to be saved. He's naked and on his back. There are hands attached to his hips. There is a tongue growing out of his neck. Lips erase his nipples. There are sighs. He's too deep inside his one room. The room starts a gentle rocking and then shifts violently. It's a hurricane and he's holding on to the wind. All around him the sheets are burning. She holds him down. He can't move from the bed as she dresses in flames.

Alias

He's late, but he knows she will wait, as he drives through a landscape tilting toward winter. When Jonah arrives she is waiting for her doll. He enters the room and sits down, moves the chair to the center of the rug, so he can be reached easily from all sides. The door is closed. Locked. They can hear the doorknob being turned, tested from the other side.

First the powder is applied. It's soft and sweet smelling. She brushes and dusts, outlines and accentuates. She is gentle but oddly nervous. He puckers his lips. A shock of watermelon red is applied then covered with apricot gloss. His short hair is teased and sprayed. A pearl clip is pinned on the right side of his head. Large emerald and ruby-colored glass earrings swing from his lobes. He will discover they get in the way of answering phone calls. He takes off his pants and shirt, but the pink prom dress can't be zipped. His chest is too large, he needs too much air just to survive. If she becomes excited, the dress would rip. The gold necklace is cold on his skin. He settles on a velvet formal. The temperature has dropped twenty degrees. Inside he's warm. She's finished and steps back smiling.

Jonah's surprised at how quickly it's over. He needs to stay in this room for hours. She for days. He turns the door knob. She steps into the hall. He watches the reactions of people she passes. He knows there's no way that she can survive. She's too flirtatious, looking up from the well of her newfound eyes, showing too much of her muscular thighs. But really she doesn't want more than to brush up against the world. She knows she is the perfect lover.

From the stares, from another woman's gasp, he wonders, is her blush too deep? Has the mascara started to run down her cheek? The necklace doesn't find a comfortable resting place on his chest. His earlobes hurt under the weight. In the mirror she's not perfect. She lifts her dress in front of the urinal. He leaves a trail of her smudged lipstick on a coffee cup. He can't take his eyes off the cup as she leaves a tip on the table. He closes the car door on the hem of her dress. She opens the door and pulls it in.

Pain in the Neck

In the gutter on an unseasonably warm December day hinting
of rain, Jonah's with two friends when Jessie walks through
him. His friends don't see that she's standing there with his
shadow. She's wearing earrings made of glass beads, of thin
wire, and tiny metal tubing that hangs down and brushes
his shoulders. When asked she describes the right one as a
one-legged woman and the left as a man with a crooked penis.
When he looks close, it's possible, although the earring woman
looks more like a European traffic sign, arms out stiff and
signaling an ever-veering one direction, and the earring man is
something closer to a furnace with a bent handle. Perhaps she's
so forthcoming because they are her perfect lovers, languidly
swaying on either side of her neck as she walks along the
street. She can be certain of everything they whisper to each
other, her head always there between them. She must know
their every yearning as a warm breath on her cheek, and how
their passion rises the faster she walks. If they ever disagree,
which is rare, he's there too, with a leg missing and an exag-
gerated organ, head cocked listening, and a stranger's shadow
at his feet.

Triathlon

Another overcast day whose beginning is the same as its end; a somber light that sinks back into shadow and grows cold deep within the streets and parks of this ancient city. It's not raining, it's not snowing, it's waiting on the edge between, to be pushed one way then the other. Looking up at the glazed half moon is to stare into the cloudy eye of the ever-changing. It's not the first time they've met, and it's certainly not an accident, unless accidents are the ever-increasing sum of inadvertent glances, the half said, the dazed feelings, and the search for something beyond quotidian collapse. The woman with one leg stands by the bed and undresses herself. She reaches behind her, elbows jutting out as if miming a naked chicken. She unhooks her bra and her breasts fill a familiar air. The man with the crooked penis sits on the bed, bent over, watching her sublime strut as he tugs at his socks.

He needs to see her naked as much as feel her naked-ness. They both slip under the blanket from opposite sides of the bed, meeting in the middle where the mattress sags and forces them together. They face each other the entire length of their skin. He proffers a kiss. She touches the arm he's not lying on. He places a hand on her waist and follows its sweep-ing curve upward. They pull each other close. She says he has her other leg. All too soon she's running with it and he's run-ning after her. It's an odd race, two people running on one leg, and the faster she runs, the faster he follows.

Sometimes it's just the daily routine, the necessary workout to stay in shape. Sometimes the path turns into the woods, crosses a creek, and ends in a mown hay field. Sometimes they head down a hill so fast they hardly touch the ground, or up a steep slope where they are left at the top panting, about to lose their one-legged balance. Sometimes they race through each other and can't remember whose leg it is. But then there are times when they stumble, can't find the rhythm of running on one leg, and then know they won't break any records. The alarm rings, Jonah rolls over, turns on the lamp, and sees Jessie's bead and wire earrings on the nightstand tangled in an odd finish.

Immolator

Every fire on Seventh Street has a face: before the panic and the
running, before any warning shouts, any singing of pain, before
speech can be shocked into recognition, before the wailing
sirens and the crowds gather to tell their versions, before anyone
can stand behind the street barricades and stare with comfort
and wander into the waning smoke of swelling tragedy.

It's exactly the moment when Jessie and Jonah rub too
hard against each other that the liquor of flames spills out
of their bodies and consumes an infinite autumn. He reels
backwards, drunk on the vision. Eyebrows ripple up into a
wavering forehead, into a mass of fiery strands that explode
above the buildings. An inflated, inflamed face stares into the
fifteenth story, melting windows, torching curtains. Its pout-
ing lip pours down the street, igniting store canopies, car tires,
newspapers, the bus stop's green bench. The scorched walls
make him whimper. Its acetylene stare sears the air. Beach-
burned, Jonah shivers in the blast of heat.

He catches his breath, the day is sunny, the only fire
is crawling under his skin. Couples with matching purple
hair stroll the Sunday sidewalk. Rollerbladers pirouette in the
middle of the street. Jessie stands beside him chatting, her face
aflame in late light. Pigeons fly out of smoldering shadows.

Sea Sea Rider

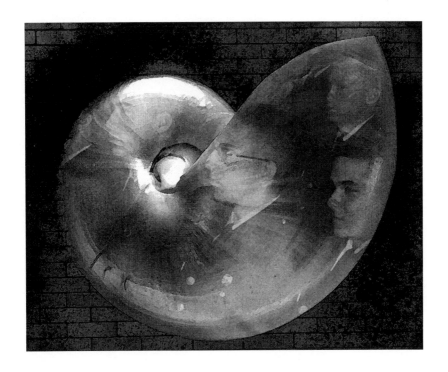

Sea of Time

It's a simple loss. Monday morning Jonah woke, thought it was Saturday, and lay there in the warmth of his own depression, blankets pulled up to his chin. He stared at the arms of the clock that kept lifting an unfathomable weight, until he heard the empty echo of the shower and knew he had to get ready for work.

This past evening, he lay down on the couch, the music from the radio rising and falling, a gentle undertow, enough to pull him under. A single small lamp casts a circle of light onto the worn-out waves of the rug. This is all it takes for him to wake to Friday and not Tuesday. It's not only sleep that misplaces days for him, in the middle of a conversation he asks the date. Told it's Wednesday, his face is all loss, a shell-shocked blankness, as if he turned his back to the street and found himself wandering the ravaged fields of Verdun nearly a century ago. He's knows his honor lies in the elegance of his defeat.

Jonah finds defeat early this morning, driving to work, when he glances along the street sees a woman hunched over in a wheelchair, a small dog sitting in her lap. He is doubled by the mirror of doubt. Should he stop, ask if she is all right? Afraid of what he will hear, he drives on, only to circle the block to see if she is still there. She is, hasn't moved, and he pulls over to the curb. He asks and can't understand the reply from the downturned face. Now he's committed to unraveling the slurred speech. It's the battery-operated wheelchair that has run down. He doesn't know how long she has sat there folded into her chair on a day of below normal temperatures with her dog in her lap. He tells her he's leaving to call the police. After he places the receiver down, he feels this happened on a different day, and he returns to the street to find the woman in the wheelchair gone.

On his birthday, when he was thirty-one, he wasn't thirty-one, he was thirty-two, but he didn't know that at the time. It didn't make sense to him for three days. In fact, he continues to search for the missing year. Its loss is a phantom limb, an itch just beyond his reach. It is hair that continues to grow around his heart, grass gone to seed on his tongue—the hulls of empty hours and days bleached pale in a ghost year. Yet he is here and there, the pulse uninterrupted in his wrist. How could this happen? He was convinced that his friends, that Jessie his wife, were simply wrong. He pulled his driver's license from his wallet. He searched for his birth certificate. He sat with pencil and paper and recalculated. He counted on his fingers as time grew more incomprehensible, a phantom amputation.

In the Candle Light Lodge the smell of disinfectant hangs in the air day and night to preserve the aged. The old man sits in a chair by the window in the light of a winter day. He doesn't move for hours. He waits in the timeless tiled corridors marred only by the call for lunch and dinner. On the wall are pastel prints of paintings with rivers and parks, the same people always picnicking on a blanket, the anemic light, the colors smeared across their faces. With a heavy Polish accent he says, "I'm too old, but I'm no different from a boy in here," and he touches his head, "but I can't even jump over the fence in the yard to save the bird from the cat. I survived a labor camp and Dresden but not this time. "

One day in New Guinea, a young Cassowary, carrying shield and spear through the jungle, walks leisurely with a visitor from far away, one who has the power to fly. The nervous visitor suggests that they hurry or they won't arrive at the village before night fall. The naked man stops, turns to say, if they walk faster the sun will set more quickly, if they take their time, the sun will match their steps.

One morning Jonah looks in the mirror, waiting for his eyes to focus, and sees the deepening shadows. He knows he will never hear the stalled traffic, the arguments, the parties, or lie down against the soft belly of that year, its light already old and bending beyond his life.

Sea of Us

The rain-filled ruts of the driveway are long reflections that lead in both directions. Each day the late summer rains arrive with the exactness of clockworks to fall on these plains. When Jonah loves the desert, he sees the tides of rising and falling over years, he sees the waves of dunes and their gritty plumes carried on the wind. He walks along their slow swelling crests, as if he were pulling off that old trick of walking on water and disappearing far out at sea. Each booted step sends a sandy avalanche down the face of an eroding wave. When he turns to look over his shoulder he sees the briefest history of the path he has followed. He hears the rattle of water's bones. Why he wonders can't he leave water alone in the earth's driest place. Why must Jonah always be drowning?

It's when he finds the certificate, among a drawer of yellowed papers, signed by the captain, recording that he crossed the Atlantic on a gray, converted World War II troop ship, that the decks are once again crowded with bawdy jokes and exaggerated bravado; edged with worry, scanning the sun-crushed sea for the ripple of a periscope; and even years later the ghosts of soldiers continue to lean shoulder to shoulder on the railings. He runs through their ragged souls to catch hold of something before the next wave strikes like a torpedo. That's how he found himself sleeping on walls and leaning on ceilings.

It was the sea that washed Jonah there. During the day it was a game. The children too distracted to be seasick waited at one end of the enclosed deck, their arms wrapped around their knees, sitting back on their heels, and when the ship desperately rose like a broken-winged bird, they'd go careening toward the far wall, exploding into laughter and arguing over who won the race. Sometimes the ship would heave so steeply, the children were a flock of sandpipers lifting off the metal deck and slamming breathlessly into the wall.

In one overwhelming wave he saw an upright tree. There were fish hanging by their tails from its branches, their gills working slowly in unison, a choir of gasping souls. Beaten by wet branches, the ship was the sea's slave. At night, alone, deep in the groaning hull, gripping the edge of the bunk, he could hear water knocking, but there was no door that would let him out, yet all doors would let the water in.

It was working hard to reach him. He could smell the sea's salty sweat. When he'd doze, his fingers loosened, and the next wave would throw him to the floor, or toss him on the wall where he would awaken, rolling toward the ceiling. In the middle of the third night he confessed to things he'd never done and came to believe in those confessions.

After the hurricane, Jonah turned his back to the vast austere sea, but it entered him. It salted his heart and wrenched it loose, collapsed its sails and guided it through the thin neck of a bottle to be set on a hearth mantel. He would never drown, even as he was daily drowning, and the one message floating out of his reach, begged to be carried by tides and washed up on an unknown beach. The gulls that had trailed them from the harbor were gone. In the quiet aftermath, he watched a ship steam along the earth's bent edge. First its black stacks appeared coughing smoke, then the wedge of its bow, but soon it rolled off into some other world. It was an event after days of a growing certainty that this was a planet of angry green waves. The only destination for the sea of us, to sail into the certainty of the next storm.

He can't leave water alone though it runs through his fingers when he bends over to test the coldness of the river. It washes over his skin as he plunges into a wave at the beach and the wind leaves him dry and crusty. He floats, a rejected lover, in a pond. In the shower one morning, sand scours the windows closed. He rinses his hair in a drizzle of quartz. The statistics are there. The taste of salt in each licked scratch.

Sea of Love

Jonah doesn't have to walk from booth to booth; the carnival comes to him. He has a lifetime pass, but he buys a ticket anyway and enters through the scalloped and scrolled wrought-iron gates. Groping through a tangle of arms, legs, and shadows to sit down, he finds the one seat still unoccupied. He is swallowed by a choir of voices from the back of the auditorium that rushes forward in waves, breaking on the edge of the stage, washing back over the crowd, resounding in an ever louder echoing cry. When the spotlight strikes the stage there is a furred silence.

A fat man, naked to the waist, head shaved and painted silver, is bathed in the beam and begins to insert plastic tubing through his nose until it reaches his stomach. Beer is pumped in with an elephantine hypodermic and then pumped out. He offers "Belly Beer" from his belly roll to slake the thirst of the multitudes rushing the stage, screaming for the elixir. This is what former Montana pharmacists do these days.

The bald Enigma, tattooed head to toe, a living jig-saw puzzle, the interlocking pieces stitched light and dark on his skin, wears a spiked choker, plays blues piano for the "Tube Man" as he awaits his turn to lift, from hooks in the bags under his eyes, the weight of the world. Near naked himself, he squints and holds his hands on both sides of his head, prepared to catch his face if it sags too far, as all seers do when they meet the future. Through the drool and snarl of it all, he's just a friendly twenty-four-year-old from the Seattle waterfront. Between acts there are maggot- and slug-eating contests, and contestants puking over the stage lights.

The "King" drops his cloak exposing hundreds of pins and nails stuck in his chest and shoulders. He stands in an immaculate light to pierce his cheeks, Adam's apple, tongue, the skin on his forehead. He raises a meat skewer and the crowd stands, a howl rising from their upturned throats. He leans his head back, the vessel of his mouth open and wanting, as the sharpened point enters. He stares straight through, his chin rises, his chest thrusts forward in the final raptured penetration. He raises his arms out from his sides. The audience esctatic, reunited in their pain.

"Mr. Lefto" in bikini underwear lifts concrete blocks with pierced nipples. He demonstrates what the body is good for: with earlobes, with tongue, with penis, the fractured world hangs from his flesh.

The ringmaster's turn: he hammers spoons up his nose, bares his back to become "The Human Dartboard," sticks his face in a box of crushed glass. A volunteer, a motherish-looking woman, bulging in every corner of her sweatsuit, stomps on the back of his head, and leans hard until he yells, "Now get the fuck off my head!" Jonah and the audience are up for a panting, oceanic ovation.

Ocean of Lonely

His hand floats in front of him, drifting out amid the crushed glare of the water, palm upturned, fingers slightly curled in the shape of a fallen maple leaf. Jonah doesn't care. He recognizes the symptoms, but then he must define a cause. He doesn't care about that either. Let's have infinite causes, he thinks, just choose one, and not necessarily the most likely one, the one we are accustomed to hearing, the one we are likely to accept, which is an empty pint of Wild Turkey lying beside him in the brown gravel, but, in fact, he decides to choose the more obtuse, the more interesting, which is a word that he has come to hate and distracts him from his boundless causality. He's ready to expel "interesting" from the language. He's ready to declare that there are no more interests, only desires, including the desire to be lonely.

What is the desire that has severed Jonah's hand from his arm and left him lying on a gravel bar? His eyes full of sun and squinting, he tries to position the bill of his cap to block the torrent of light. Maybe, if he pulls his arm back toward him, away from the creek, his hand will follow. He's not ready to act decisively and continues to examine his outstretched arm, surrounded by swirling current. It's heavy as a submerged log. His entire body is sinking below time. He can't understand how so much can disappear and still be in sight. He follows from his feet up to his shoulder, his dissembling into another tumbled drunk piece of chert warming on a spring day on a gravel bar midcreek. When he stops listening to water's endless breaking, and he stands, his head fills with the rattle of stones. He stumbles a little farther into a blue and perfectly empty sky. He looks for the right shape and size. Jonah's hand spins in an eddy at the end of his wrist as he flings a flat stone. It water-walks, skips, skims, sinks.

Mansion With One Sea

This is not Jonah's room. The door is cracked open. Maybe
they don't want him to fall through the darkness forever. It's
the quickest way to get him to stop crying, to fall asleep, throw
him a splinter of light. There's someone in the other bed. For
her sleep happens here every night. Her slow breathing is a
broom sweeping a far corner in yet another room.

One night he looked into his parent's bedroom, and
there was no one in bed. The chenille bedspread was smooth,
pulled over the fluffed pillows, as if clouds had gathered
against the headboard. He walked to the front door and out
of the apartment, down the stairwell and into the basement.
He walked under the street. No one saw him. He followed a
river of rumors to the next building and knocked on the door
of the apartment where friends of his parents lived. They
answered and told him to go home, it was three o'clock in the
morning.

Jonah heard the city's stark hum threatening to drown
him. He noticed how the streetlights, the parking lot, the
buildings, the man sitting on the curb staring up at nothing
that he could see, were balanced on night's thick stalk. His
parents were waiting at the door when he returned. They
tucked him back into bed and said he'd been sleepwalking.
In the morning, he walked past their bedroom and looked in.
The bedspread was smooth, pulled up over the pillows, as if a
rain had washed them clean of sleep.

He pulls the covers over his head, listens to a breathing
that doesn't tire of cleaning out then cluttering a distant room.
He begins to count each rasping sweep of the broom. The
rough handle rattles as it hits the floor. When the wood snaps
in her chest, his own breath catches.

He wants to get up but he can't move his arms or legs.
Something is holding him down. He's not big enough, to lift
so much night off his face. Maybe it's the light slicing through
the crack in the door, maybe the laughter on the other side
that gives him strength. He walks into the kitchen. There are
adults exposing so much. There is laughter before the adults

catch sight of him in his pajamas. Jonah's quickly taken back to the room. The sweeping begins again. He can't catch up to the broom. Far back in the other corner, the handle breaks into shorter and shorter pieces.

Walter Bargen's work has appeared in his 12 books, and over one hundred magazines, including *The Georgia Review, Beloit Poetry Journal,* and *Prairie Schooner.* The first poet laureate of Missouri, he is the recipient of a National Endowment for the Arts fellowship in poetry, and winner of the William Rockhill Nelson Award. Other awards include the *Quarter After Eight* Prose Prize (for the "Nine Lives on the Western Front" sequence in this book), the St. Louis Poetry Center's Hanks Prize, and the Chester H. Jones Foundation Prize. He lives in Ashland, Missouri.

Mike Sleadd teaches in the Art Department at Columbia College in Columbia, Missouri. Known primarily for his intricate pen and ink drawings, this is the first book that he has illustrated using digital images.